THE BRITISH OVERSEAS

a guide to records
of their births, baptisms,
marriages, deaths and burials,
available in the United Kingdom

COMPILED BY
GEOFFREY YEO

GUILDHALL LIBRARY
SECOND EDITION
1988

Guildhall Library Publications
Guildhall Library, Aldermanbury, London.

ISBN 0 900422 26 2

First published 1984
Second edition 1988

Copyright © Guildhall Library

Printed in Britain by
Manor Park Press Limited, England.

CONTENTS

	Page
How to use this guide	1
Addresses of English repositories mentioned in the guide	2
Printed sources	2
Abbreviations used	2
Acknowledgements	3
Part I: Introduction to the sources	4
Records of English baptisms, marriages and burials in churches and chapels overseas	4
'International memoranda' of baptisms, marriages and burials overseas, at Guildhall Library	6
Civil registration records of births, marriages and deaths of English residents in foreign countries (from 1849), at St Catherine's House	6
Civil registration records in Empire and Commonwealth countries	7
Foreign office records at the Public Record Office, Kew	7
Non-statutory records at the Public Record Office, Chancery Lane	8
Records of military units abroad and ships at sea	9
Records of the Scots, Irish and Welsh overseas	10
Other related sources	11
Emigration records	11
Wills	11
Monumental inscriptions	12
The Mormon International Genealogical Index	12
The Society of Genealogists	12
Sources available outside the United Kingdom	13
Part II: List of known registers for individual places overseas	15-72

HOW TO USE THIS GUIDE
What it includes

This *Guide* is to sources which may be used to trace the births (or baptisms), marriages and deaths (or burials) of British persons overseas, occurring before c.1945. Some post-1945 sources are mentioned, but for more detailed information about this period enquiries should be made at the General Register Office, St Catherine's House, Kingsway, London WC2, where almost all the available records are held.

The *Guide* is primarily to sources available in the United Kingdom. Some material held in other countries is mentioned, but no attempt has been made at comprehensive coverage.

How to trace a particular person or family

1. Consult list of sources for individual countries (pages 15-72).
2. If this does not provide the information required, consult, as appropriate:
   (a) English and Welsh civil registration records of births, marriages and deaths in foreign countries (i.e. outside the British Empire or Commonwealth), from 1849, at St Catherine's House, Kingsway, London WC2 (see page 6); or similar Scottish and Irish civil registration records (see page 11).
   (b) 'Miscellaneous' series 1826-1951 at the Public Record Office, Chancery Lane, London WC2 (see page 8).
   (c) Various sources for events at sea and persons serving in military units abroad (see pages 9-10).
3. If more guidance is needed, read the detailed introduction to the background and nature of the sources (pages 4-12).
4. If the above sources do not provide the information required, it will be necessary to search for records held outside the United Kingdom (see pages 13-14).

ADDRESSES OF ENGLISH REPOSITORIES MENTIONED IN THE GUIDE

Baptist Missionary Society, 93-7 Gloucester Place, London W1H 4AA.
Borthwick Institute of Historical Research, St Anthony's Hall, Peasholme Green, York YO1 2PW.
British Library, Great Russell Street, London WC1B 3DG.
Church Missionary Society, 157 Waterloo Road, London SE1 8UU.
Genealogical Libraries of the Church of Jesus Christ of Latter-Day Saints, 64-8 Exhibition Road, London SW7 2PA (and other addresses in various countries).
Greater London Record Office, 40 Northampton Road, London EC1R 0HB.
Guildhall Library, Aldermanbury, London EC2P 2EJ.
India Office Library and Records, 197 Blackfriars Road, London SE1 8NG.
Lambeth Palace Library, London SE1 7JU.
Principal Probate Registry (Principal Registry of the Family Division), Somerset House, London WC2R 1LP.
Public Record Office, Chancery Lane, London WC2A 1LR.
Public Record Office, Ruskin Avenue, Kew, Surrey TW9 4DU.
St Catherine's House (General Register Office), Kingsway, London WC2B 6JP.
School of Oriental and African Studies, Malet Street, London WC1E 7HP.
Society for Promoting Christian Knowledge, Holy Trinity Church, Marylebone Road, London NW1 4DU.
Society of Genealogists, 14 Charterhouse Buildings, London EC1M 7BA.
United Society for the Propagation of the Gospel: archives now held by The Librarian, Rhodes House Library, South Parks Road, Oxford OX1 3RG.

PRINTED SOURCES

Printed books and other publications mentioned in the *Guide* are available for consultation at Guildhall Library unless otherwise stated. They can also generally be seen at the Society of Genealogists and/or the British Library.

ABBREVIATIONS USED

Bap: baptism(s)
Bur: burial(s)
c.: circa
Mar: marriage(s)
PRO: Public Record Office
Vol: volume(s)

ACKNOWLEDGEMENTS

Assistance in the compilation of the *Guide* has been received from many people, including the staff of most of the repositories holding overseas registers. Particular thanks are due to my present and former colleagues at Guildhall Library, to Mr Anthony Camp and Mr L. W. Lawson Edwards of the Society of Genealogists and to Mr Gerry Toop of the Public Record Office.

The holdings of Guildhall Library are described as at 1 August 1986, and those of other repositories from information supplied between 1977 and 1986.

Geoffrey Yeo
September 1986

PART I
INTRODUCTION TO THE SOURCES
RECORDS OF ENGLISH BAPTISMS, MARRIAGES AND BURIALS IN CHURCHES AND CHAPELS OVERSEAS

Churches in non-English-speaking countries

Anglican churches were established in many European towns from the 17th century onwards. In some towns English non-conformist churches were also established. Before this, in France, Germany, the Netherlands and Switzerland, the baptisms, marriages and burials of Anglican and English non-conformist residents were commonly recorded in the registers of local protestant churches. This practice probably continued at later dates in areas where there was no convenient English church. It appears that such entries are particularly numerous in the protestant registers of Angers, Bordeaux, Caen, Nantes, Saumur, Tours, Basle, Frankfurt, Geneva, Rotterdam, Strasbourg and Zurich.* These registers are of course kept in their country of origin, usually at the church in question or in a local record repository. It is not known what arrangements were made by Anglicans and non-conformists in countries where there were no protestant churches. English Roman Catholics overseas should be sought in the baptism, marriage and burial registers of local Roman Catholic churches.

When English churches were established in Europe, they began to maintain their own registers. The earliest known is that of the Anglican church at Hamburg, which begins in 1617. A few other 17th century registers exist, but for most English churches in Europe the surviving records do not begin until the 18th or (more commonly) the 19th century.

There are also some registers for churches in non-English-speaking countries outside Europe, though few were established before the 19th century. It is not known what arrangements were made by English residents in countries where there was no English church. Some baptisms, marriages and burials may have been entered in the registers of other churches, while some are likely to have remained unrecorded.

Where Anglican or other 'English' churches existed overseas, they are likely to have been used on occasion by others besides English people. Thus the registers of Anglican churches may include baptisms, marriages and burials of Welsh, Scottish, Irish or colonial Anglicans. Mixed marriages (i.e. where one party was a foreign national), and baptisms of the children of such marriages, may be found either in local protestant or Roman Catholic registers or in those of Anglican or English non-conformist churches.

---

*J. S. Burn, *The History of Parish Registers* . . . (London, 1862), page 241; N. Currer-Briggs, *Worldwide Family History* (London, 1982), page 28; *National Index of Parish Registers*, vol 2 (Chichester, 1973), pages 763-7.

Many Anglican registers have been forwarded to the United Kingdom for safe keeping (see below), but few records of non-conformist churches overseas are available for consultation here.

Churches in former British colonies
Anglican churches were established in overseas colonial territories from the 17th century onwards. However the registers of these churches were very rarely sent to England, and in most cases must be sought in the country concerned.

Records held in the United Kingdom
The records of overseas churches which are available for consultation in the United Kingdom fall into three categories: (a) original registers which have been brought to the United Kingdom; (b) copies made for official purposes, e.g. 'bishop's transcripts'; (c) published and unpublished transcripts or photographic copies made by researchers. Many Anglican registers in categories (a) and (b) are at Guildhall Library as part of the archives of the Bishop of London, who was held to exercise responsibility for Anglican churches overseas where no other bishop had been appointed;* further registers can be found at PRO Chancery Lane, Lambeth Palace Library and various other repositories. Details are given on pages 15-72.

Records held outside the United Kingdom
Considerable numbers of records remain in the custody of individual churches or in archive repositories overseas. Possible means of tracing them are suggested on pages 13-14.

*For the origins and legal status of the Bishop of London's jurisdiction overseas, see the introduction to W. W. Manross, *The Fulham Papers in Lambeth Palace Library* (Oxford, 1965). The Bishop of London retained responsibility for churches in north and central Europe until 1980, but his jurisdiction in southern Europe ceased in 1842 on the creation of the diocese of Gibraltar. The allegiance of the American (Episcopal) church to the Bishop of London came to an end after American independence in 1776. The first Anglican bishop in Canada was appointed in 1787, and the other British colonies generally acquired bishops of their own in the 19th century. This explains why registers from colonial territories are not generally found in the Bishop of London's archives. However records of baptisms, marriages and burials in India were returned to the civil authorities and are now at the India Office Library in London: see page 35.

'INTERNATIONAL MEMORANDA' OF BAPTISMS, MARRIAGES AND BURIALS OVERSEAS, AT GUILDHALL LIBRARY

In the 19th and early 20th centuries the Bishop of London's registry maintained a series of volumes (now known as 'International memoranda') for the registration of miscellaneous foreign baptisms, marriages and burials. Most of the entries are for baptisms and marriages by chaplains officiating at British embassies abroad, but the series includes a number of other registrations made, e.g., by clergymen travelling overseas or on board ship.*

Registrations were sometimes accepted up to thirty years after a baptism, marriage or burial. Thus, although the first registration was accepted in 1816, the earliest baptism recorded in the series took place in 1788. The 'International memoranda' are Guildhall Library Ms.10,926/1-13.

1. 1816-24　⎫　　　　　　　　7. 1865-9　　⎫
2. 1824-32　⎪ including　　　 8. 1869-72　⎪ including
3. 1832-40　⎬ baptisms,　　　 9. 1872-5　　⎬ baptisms,
4. 1840- 6　⎪ marriages　　 10. 1875-8　　⎪ marriages
5. 1847-57　⎪ & burials　　　11. 1878-83　⎪ & burials
6. 1857-65　⎭ up to 30 years 12. 1883-9　 ⎭ up to 5 years
　　　　　　　earlier　　　　 13. 1889-1924 earlier

Ms.10,926/1-10 may be consulted only on microfilm.

Indexes are kept on the open shelves in the Manuscripts reading room at Guildhall Library: Ms.10,926C/1-2. For *details of the countries covered* in this series see pages 15-72.

CIVIL REGISTRATION RECORDS OF BIRTHS, MARRIAGES AND DEATHS OF ENGLISH RESIDENTS IN FOREIGN COUNTRIES (FROM 1849), AT ST CATHERINE'S HOUSE

The Acts of Parliament of 1836 and 1837, which established a system of civil registration of births, marriages and deaths in England and Wales, did not apply to persons of British nationality outside the United Kingdom. Statutory civil registration records of English births, marriages and deaths which occurred in foreign countries do not begin until 1849.** Since that date records of births and deaths which were known to British consuls and legations in foreign countries (i.e. outside the British Empire or Commonwealth) have been returned by them to the Registrar General in London, in accordance with Foreign Office instructions. Civil registration records of marriages solemnized or attended by British consuls in foreign countries are kept under the terms of the Consular Marriages Act 1849, and later enactments, which required that marriage registers should be maintained by each consul,

---

*For registrations at sea, see also page 9.
**For Irish and Scottish births, marriages and deaths see page 11.

and that certified copies thereof should be returned to the Registrar General. The Act of 1849 allowed for civil marriages to be conducted by the consuls themselves, but also covered marriages solemnized in the consul's presence by a clergyman of the Church of England or by any other person. Marriages conducted by a foreign minister under the marriage laws of the country concerned were known as *lex loci* marriages and were sometimes entered by consuls in separate registers; copies of these were also returned to the Registrar General. It is probable that many births, marriages and deaths in foreign countries, particularly in the 19th century, were unknown to the British consuls and were therefore not registered in this way; but the more recent records are likely to be more comprehensive.

Access to the records
All the above statutory (or 'consular') records of births, marriages and deaths in foreign countries are now kept with the Registrar General's civil registration records for England and Wales at St Catherine's House, where the indexes are available for public consultation.

Certificates may be obtained there on payment of the appropriate fee.

CIVIL REGISTRATION RECORDS IN EMPIRE AND COMMONWEALTH COUNTRIES

The records at St Catherine's House do not cover places which were part of the British Empire or Commonwealth at the time when the birth, marriage or death occurred. Residents in British colonies or dominions were subject to the registration laws in operation in the locality concerned, and records of their births, deaths and marriages were kept locally rather than being returned to London.

Possible means of tracing these records are suggested on page 13.

FOREIGN OFFICE RECORDS AT THE PUBLIC RECORD OFFICE, KEW

A number of documents previously kept at British consulates abroad are available for public consultation among the Foreign Office records (class FO) at PRO Kew. These include some of the original registers of births, marriages and deaths from which the consuls' returns to the Registrar General were compiled; it should be noted, however, that they do not represent the whole of the coverage of the Registrar General's records of overseas registration held at St Catherine's House. The Foreign Office records also contain a number of registers of baptisms and burials, whose contents are apparently not duplicated elsewhere; and much other material relating to British residents overseas, including registers of passports issued at consulates, lists of British subjects in various towns overseas, and papers relating to the wills and estates of British expatriates, mainly from the late 19th and early 20th centuries.

Details of the Foreign Office registers of births, baptisms, marriages, deaths and burials (including those whose contents are duplicated at St Catherine's House) are given in the list on pages 15-72 of this *Guide*. For other Foreign Office material the enquirer is advised to consult the *Current Guide to the Contents of the Public Record Office* (PRO microfiche publication) and the typewritten lists in the search rooms at PRO Kew (some of which have been published by the Kraus Reprint Corporation, New York, various dates). Access to the records is subject to a 30-year (in some cases 50-year) closure period.

NON-STATUTORY RECORDS AT THE PUBLIC RECORD OFFICE, CHANCERY LANE

Besides the statutory records described on pages 6-7, the Registrar General also had custody, until 1977, of a number of non-statutory registers of births, baptisms, marriages, deaths and burials overseas. These have now been transferred to PRO Chancery Lane, where they form five series known as 'Miscellaneous Foreign Returns' (RG32), 'Foreign Registers and Returns' (RG33), 'Miscellaneous Foreign Marriages' (RG34), 'Miscellaneous Foreign Deaths' (RG35) and 'Registers and Returns of Births, Marriages and Deaths in Protectorates etc . . .' (RG36).

Each of the registers in RG33 relates to a particular locality, and details of the places and dates covered are given in the list on pages 15-72. Details of RG36 will also be found on pages 15-72. Indexes to RG33 and RG36 are kept on the open shelves in the 'Long Room' at PRO Chancery Lane.

The 'Miscellaneous' series 1826-1951
The 'Miscellaneous' registers which comprise RG32, RG34 and RG35 contain numerous entries from all parts of the world between 1826 and 1951, and their contents have not been analysed in detail on pages 15-72. Most of the entries are from 'foreign' countries, but some Empire and Commonwealth registrations are included. Indexes to entries made before 1946 (except military deaths 1914-21) are also kept in the 'Long Room' at PRO Chancery Lane, as follows:

Births & bap 1831-1930: RG43/2   Deaths & bur 1830-81: RG43/4
Mar 1826-1916: RG43/8   Deaths & bur 1881-1900: RG43/5
Mar 1913-20: RG43/9   Deaths & bur 1901-20: RG43/6
Births, bap, mar, deaths & bur 1921-45: RG43/10-14.

RECORDS OF MILITARY UNITS ABROAD AND SHIPS AT SEA*

The Army and Royal Air Force
Records of births, marriages and deaths (also some baptisms and burials) in Army regiments at home and abroad are at St Catherine's House.** The records cover 1761-date for regiments based in England, but the earliest overseas entry is c.1790. From 1920 entries relating to the Royal Air Force are also included. The records are known as 'Regimental registers', with additional series known as 'Army returns' and 'Chaplains' returns'.

A few further records of baptisms, marriages and burials by Forces chaplains abroad are held elsewhere, viz.:

Cape of Good Hope garrison, bap 1795-1803, mar 1796-1803, bur 1795-1803: Guildhall Library, Ms. 11,569.

Germany, British Army on the Rhine, civilian bap 1949-61 and 1969-76: Guildhall Library, Ms. 11,225-5B.

Gibraltar garrison, bap and mar 1807-12, bur 1807: Guildhall Library, Ms. 10,446D.

Palestine forces, bap 1939-47, banns 1944-7: PRO Kew, WO156/6-8.

Some military baptisms, marriages and burials may be entered in non-military registers (for which see pages 15-72).

Ships at sea (Merchant vessels and Royal Navy)
Births and deaths on board merchant vessels may be recorded in the log of the ship concerned. However few ships' logs survive from before the mid 19th century. Some are at PRO Kew, but it is practicable to search them only if the name of the ship is known.

However from 1837 to date records of English births and deaths at sea returned by captains of merchant vessels and Royal Navy ships are at St Catherine's House.*** These records are indexed. They are known as 'Marine births' and 'Marine deaths'. There are also records of births 1854-91, marriages 1854-83 and deaths 1854-90 of seamen and passengers on merchant ships at PRO Kew (class BT 158-60). Later records are held by the Registry of Shipping and Seamen, Llantrisant Road, Llandaff, Cardiff CF5 2YS. Marriages 1842-89 on Royal Navy ships are recorded at PRO Chancery Lane (class RG33/156; index in RG43/7); for the period 1842-79 these marriages are also registered in the 'International memoranda' at Guildhall Library (see page 6).

Guildhall Library also has records of some baptisms and burials at sea

---

*For wills of soldiers and sailors see pages 11-12.
**The garrison registers listed on pages 185-6 of *Abstract of arrangements respecting registration of births, marriages and deaths in the United Kingdom and the other countries of the British Commonwealth* . . . (HMSO, 1952) form part of these records. Some names from the garrison registers appear in the index volumes kept in the Long Room at PRO Chancery Lane but the registers themselves remain at St Catherine's House.

***For similar records relating to Irish and Scottish births and deaths see page 11.

1894-1952 (Ms. 11,827), and baptisms at sea 1955-61 (Ms. 11,817; index in Ms. 15,061/1-2, under 'sea'). There are some further baptisms, 1810, 1822 and 1860-1921, and burials, 1860-1919, at sea in the 'International memoranda' at Guildhall Library (see page 6).

The popular belief that all baptisms at sea were registered at St Dunstan Stepney is incorrect*; however there are some baptisms at sea from 1893 entered in the registers of that church, which are held by the Greater London Record Office. The records there include baptisms for the Mediterranean fleet at Malta 1933-8.

Registers of baptisms and burials in the Naval dockyard at Bermuda 1826-1946 are at PRO Kew (class ADM 6).

War deaths

Deaths of military personnel overseas in the Boer War 1899-1902, First World War 1914-21 and Second World War 1939-48 are recorded and indexed at St Catherine's House. Printed sources which may also be relevant include, for the First World War, *The War Graves of the British Empire, 1914-18*, and for the Second World War, *The War Dead of the British Commonwealth, 1939-45*, both published by the Commonwealth War Graves Commission. Guildhall Library also has copies of the War Office's official lists of officers and soldiers who died in the First World War, arranged by regiment.

RECORDS OF THE SCOTS, IRISH AND WELSH OVERSEAS

Church records

Baptisms, marriages and burials overseas of persons of Scottish, Irish or Welsh origin who were members of the Anglican church or of a British non-conformist sect (e.g. the Methodist church) should be sought in the records of the appropriate 'English' church, if there was one: see pages 4-5. Those who were members of the Roman Catholic church should be sought in the registers of local Roman Catholic churches in the country concerned.

Some records of Church of Scotland (Presbyterian) churches abroad have been returned to the United Kingdom: details are given in the list on pages 15-72. Information about other records should be sought from the churches themselves. The addresses of individual churches can be obtained from the Church of Scotland Overseas Council, 121 George Street, Edinburgh EH2 4YN.

---

*See A. D. Ridge, 'All at Sea', in *Archives* vol 6 (1964).

Civil registration records: Scottish
Civil records of Scottish births and deaths overseas, and of marriages overseas where one or both parties were of Scottish origin, from 1860, and civil records of Scottish births and deaths at sea from 1855, are held at the General Register Office, New Register House, Edinburgh EH1 3YT.

Civil registration records: Irish
Civil records of Irish births and deaths certified by British consuls abroad, and of Irish births and deaths at sea, 1864-1921, are held at the General Register Office, 8-11 Lombard Street East, Dublin 2. Similar records for Northern Irish births and deaths, commencing in 1922, are at the General Register Office, Oxford House, Chichester Street, Belfast BT1 4HL.

Civil registration records: Welsh
There are no separate civil records of Welsh births, marriages and deaths overseas. They are included in the records of English civil registration described on pages 6-7.

OTHER RELATED SOURCES
Emigration records
The Public Record Office (Kew and Chancery Lane) has a large number of unpublished sources relating to emigration from Britain, particularly emigration to North America, the West Indies, Australia and New Zealand in the 18th and 19th centuries. Records relating to the transportation of convicts from Britain are also held there. A leaflet giving details of these sources is available at the Public Record Office (leaflet 7).

Surviving records of immigrants at foreign ports of arrival are generally kept in the National Archives in the country concerned. Its address can usually be obtained from the latest edition of *The World of Learning* (Europa Publications, London). In some countries, notably Australia and South Africa, immigration records are kept in State or Provincial Archives.

A number of emigrant ship passenger lists, and lists of early settlers in the American, South African and Australasian colonies, have been published. For the United States, Canada and the West Indies, P. W. Filby and M. K. Meyer, *Passenger and immigration lists index* and *Passenger and immigration lists bibliography 1538-1900* (Detroit, 1981-5) will be found especially useful. The Society of Genealogists has a large collection of published work of this kind (for Australasia and South Africa as well as America).

Wills
Wills of Englishmen dying abroad or at sea but in possession of goods in England were generally proved, until 1858, in the Prerogative Court of

Canterbury. The records of this court are at PRO Chancery Lane; they include wills of soldiers and sailors besides those of civilians dying abroad.

Such wills were occasionally proved, until 1858, in other courts. The will of an individual dying abroad whose property was wholly within one English diocese may sometimes be found in the records of a probate court in that diocese: for a list of such courts and their records see A. Camp, *Wills and their Whereabouts* (London, 1974). The records of the Prerogative Court of York, held at the Borthwick Institute of Historical Research in York, also include many persons dying abroad with property in the north of England.

Enquiries about wills of persons dying abroad with property in England after 1858 should be made to the Principal Probate Registry at Somerset House.

Wills of persons dying abroad with property in Scotland are to be found in the records of the Commissariot of Edinburgh. These records (pre-1960) are at the Scottish Record Office, H. M. General Register House, Edinburgh EH1 3YY.

From the late 17th century there are many wills of seamen on merchant vessels (to 1857), and some on ships of the Royal Navy (to c.1750), in the records of the Commissary Court of London (London division) at Guildhall Library. These records also include some wills of soldiers dying abroad (c.1790-c.1830).

Original wills of seamen in the Royal Navy 1786-1882 are at PRO Kew (class ADM48).

Monumental inscriptions
A number of transcripts of inscriptions from graveyards overseas exist in published or unpublished form. The largest collection is at the Society of Genealogists.

The Mormon International Genealogical Index
This index, compiled by the Church of Jesus Christ of Latter-Day Saints, includes numerous persons baptised and married in many countries throughout the world. There is a separate part of the index for each country. The parts for countries outside the British Isles are not available at Guildhall Library, but may be seen at the Society of Genealogists or at the Genealogical Libraries of the Church of Jesus Christ of Latter-Day Saints.

The Society of Genealogists
The Society of Genealogists holds numerous books and periodicals relating to various aspects of overseas genealogy and the activities of English communities abroad. Many of them are not readily available elsewhere in the United Kingdom. By no means all contain biographical details about named individuals, but even those which do not may be found useful in providing background information and in suggesting further lines of enquiry.

SOURCES AVAILABLE OUTSIDE THE UNITED KINGDOM

Records held by civil registration authorities
Civil registration records of births, marriages and deaths kept locally outside the United Kingdom may include details of British residents in the country concerned. Details of such records kept in Commonwealth countries can be found in *Abstract of arrangements respecting registration of births, marriages and deaths in the United Kingdom and the other countries of the British Commonwealth* . . . (HMSO, 1952). The addresses of some registration authorities have changed since the publication of *Abstract of arrangements* . . ., and a more up-to-date list of their addresses can be found in *Fees for searches and certificates of events occurring outside England and Wales* (General Register Office, 1967). This booklet is not available at Guildhall Library, but an annotated copy can be seen on request at St Catherine's House. The staff of the Overseas Registration Section at St Catherine's House can also supply the current addresses of registration authorities in non-Commonwealth countries, and advise on the procedure for making enquiries to these authorities.

Civil registration was introduced at different times in different countries overseas. In most countries the records go back to the 19th century but in some countries civil registration was not introduced, or made comprehensive, until the 20th century. However in a number of countries the civil registration authorities are also able to provide information about church registers and any other sources which pre-date the introduction of civil registration.

Records held in archive repositories
In some countries church registers are now in the custody of public archive repositories. Such repositories are most likely to have custody of the records of those churches to which the bulk of the local population belonged. Records of 'English' churches in non-English-speaking countries are less likely to be found in archive repositories abroad. However such repositories may be able to provide information about the whereabouts of surviving church registers even if these are not in their own custody.

The addresses of National Archives in overseas countries can usually be obtained from the latest edition of *The World of Learning* (Europa Publications, London). However church registers are often held in provincial, state or other local repositories, whose addresses should be sought from the National Archives or from the London embassy or high commission of the country concerned.

Records held in churches
Many churches overseas retain custody of their own registers, and in such cases information should be sought from the incumbent or minister of the church in question. A booklet giving addresses of Anglican and other English churches in Europe, North Africa and the Middle East

can be purchased from the Intercontinental Church Society, 175 Tower Bridge Road, London SE1. For Anglican churches outside these areas, addresses may be obtainable from the diocesan authorities in the country concerned; details of Anglican dioceses overseas can be found in the latest edition of *The Church of England Year Book* (CIO Publishing, London). Similar publications are available for most other major denominations. They are not held at Guildhall Library but may be consulted nearby at the City Business Library, 55 Basinghall Street, London EC2V 5BX, and at many other public reference libraries. It should be noted, however, that an enquiry to the church authorities about a particular baptism, marriage or burial, is unlikely to be successful if the church where it took place is not known to the enquirer.

PART II

LIST OF KNOWN REGISTERS FOR INDIVIDUAL PLACES OVERSEAS

With a few exceptions, this list refers only to registers of British communities overseas which are available for consultation in the United Kingdom. It is arranged alphabetically by name of country, such names being given as far as possible in the form in common English use after the end of the Second World War, with cross-references from earlier or later names. Names of cities and towns are indicated where possible (though the register for a city or town is likely to include surrounding villages, and frequently a much wider area); dedications of churches are not given. In most cases no attempt has been made to distinguish unpublished transcripts from original registers.

Dates given in the list are covering dates only. It is rarely clear whether gaps in a series represent periods when no registrations were made, or are the result of loss or neglect. In some instances the dates given may be those when births, etc., were registered by an appropriate authority; in such cases the birth itself may have taken place at an earlier date. When an overlap of covering dates is found in the list, it will be advisable to examine all the sources mentioned, as there were often separate registers kept by different officials or clergymen in the same locality.

The list does not include the statutory 'consular' registers 1849-date (see pages 6-7 and 11); and does not give a full analysis of the 'miscellaneous' series 1826-1951 at PRO Chancery Lane (see page 8), or of the various general series for military units abroad and ships at sea (see pages 9-10).

ADEN (SOUTH YEMEN)

Births, mar and deaths 1839-43: printed in *East India Register* 1840-4 (under 'Bombay').

Births, mar and deaths 1839-82: printed in *Bombay Directory* 1840-83 (not available at Guildhall Library).

Bap, mar and bur 1840-1969: India Office Library, N/13/1-21.

ALGERIA

Many entries among registrations for France and its colonies in 'Miscellaneous' series 1826-1951 at PRO Chancery Lane (see page 8).

For addresses of repositories see page 2

For other sources which may relate to places on this page see 'How to use this guide' (page 1)

ANGOLA
Luanda
Births 1865-1906, mar 1871-1928, deaths 1859-1906: PRO Kew, FO375/1-4.

ANGUILLA: see WEST INDIES

ANTIGUA: see WEST INDIES

ARGENTINA
General
Some entries for bap 1815-41, mar 1813-95 in 'International memoranda' at Guildhall Library: see page 6.

Buenos Aires
Mar 1826-1900: PRO Kew, FO446/3-6, 28-30.
Bap and mar 1909-46: Society of Genealogists.

ASCENSION ISLAND
Bap 1839-61, mar 1840-59, deaths 1839-61: Society of Genealogists.

Bap 1846, mar 1847-56 in 'International memoranda' at Guildhall Library: see page 6.

AUSTRALIA
General
Microfiche copies of indexes to *New South Wales* bap 1790-1856, births 1856-99, mar 1789-1899 and bur 1787-1899; *Queensland* bap 1829-56, mar 1839-99, bur 1829-56 and deaths 1856-99; *South Australia* births, mar and deaths 1842-1906; *Victoria* births, mar and deaths 1837-95; *Western Australia* births, mar and deaths 1841-96; are available at the Society of Genealogists. The original records are held locally in Australia, and enquiries about them should be addressed to the Registrar of the appropriate Australian state, at the following addresses:
    New South Wales: The Registrar of Births, Deaths and Marriages, Prince Albert Road, Sydney 2000, Australia.
    Queensland: The Registrar General, Old Treasury Building,

---

For addresses of repositories see page 2

For other sources which may relate to places on this page see 'How to use this guide' (page 1)

Brisbane 4000, Australia.
South Australia: The Principal Registrar, G.P.O. Box 1351H, Adelaide 5001, Australia.
Tasmania: The Registrar General, Box 129, North Hobart 7002, Australia.
Victoria: The Government Statist, 295 Queen Street, Melbourne 3000, Australia.
Western Australia: The Registrar General, Oakleigh Building, 22 St George's Terrace, Perth 6000, Australia.

For records of emigration to Australia see page 11.

For further information about Australian sources see N. T. Hansen, *Guide to Genealogical Sources in Australia and New Zealand* (Melbourne, 1963). Assistance may also be obtained from the Society of Australian Genealogists, Richmond Villa, 120 Kent Street, Observatory Hill, Sydney 2000.

Albury
Bap 1911 in 'International memoranda' at Guildhall Library: see page 6.

Brisbane
Mar 1868-72: Society of Genealogists.

Bunbury
Bur 1840-52: Society of Genealogists.

New South Wales
Index to mar 1788-1800: Society of Genealogists.

Prospect
Bap 1841-88, mar 1841-56, bur 1841-88: Society of Genealogists.

Wellington District
Mar 1839-51: Society of Genealogists.

AUSTRIA
General
Some entries for bap 1821-1902, mar 1849-91, bur 1849 in 'International memoranda' at Guildhall Library: see page 6.

For addresses of repositories see page 2

For other sources which may relate to places on this page see 'How to use this guide' (page 1)

Innsbruck
Bur 1957: Guildhall Library, in Ms. 21,477.

Vienna
Mar 1883-91: PRO Kew, FO120/697.

AZORES: see PORTUGAL

BAHAMAS: see WEST INDIES

BALEARIC ISLANDS: see SPAIN

BANGLADESH: see INDIA

BARBADOS: see WEST INDIES

BELGIUM
General
Many entries in 'Miscellaneous' series 1826-1951 at PRO Chancery Lane (see page 8); the series also includes separate death registers for Belgium 1830-71 (RG35/1-3) and 1914-21 (military deaths only; incomplete) (RG35/45-57).
Some entries for bap 1815-48, mar 1815-90 in 'International memoranda' at Guildhall Library: see page 6.

Antwerp
Bap 1817-52, mar 1820-49, bur 1817-52: PRO Chancery Lane, RG33/1-2 (index to bap in RG43/1, mar in RG43/7, bur in RG43/3).
Bap 1819-30, mar 1821-30, bur 1819-30: Guildhall Library, Ms. 11,198 (index in Ms. 15,061/1-2).
Bap 1831-42, mar 1832-42, bur 1831-42: PRO Chancery Lane, in RG33/155 (index to bap in RG43/1, mar in RG43/7, bur in RG43/3).

Brussels
Bap, mar and bur 1818-26: Guildhall Library, Ms. 11,199 (index in Ms. 15,061/1-2).
Mar 1816-90: PRO Chancery Lane, RG33/3-8 (index in RG43/7).

For addresses of repositories see page 2

For other sources which may relate to places on this page see 'How to use this guide' (page 1)

Ghent
Mar 1849-50: PRO Chancery Lane, RG33/9 (index in RG43/7).

Liège
Bap 1823-5: Guildhall Library, in Ms. 11,219 (index in Ms. 15,061/1-2).

Ostend
Bap 1784-7, mar and bur 1784-6: Guildhall Library, Ms. 10,457/1 (index in Ms. 15,061/1-2).
Bap 1787-94: Guildhall Library, Ms. 10,457/2 (index in Ms. 15,061/1-2).
Mar 1787-94: Guildhall Library, Ms. 10,457/3 (index in Ms. 15,061/1-2).
Bur 1787-94: Guildhall Library, Ms. 10,457/4 (index in Ms. 15,061/1-2).
Military bap, mar and bur 1815-16: extracts printed in *The Genealogist* vol 1 (1877). The original vol from which these extracts were taken is now part of the Registrar General's military records at St Catherine's House (see page 9).

BERMUDA

Bap 1812-30, mar 1812-48, bur 1812-15: printed in *Miscellanea Genealogica et Heraldica* New series vol 4 (1884).

British naval dockyard bap and bur 1826-1946: PRO Kew, ADM6/434-6, 439.

Enquiries about other records (from 1619) should be addressed to the Bermuda Archives, Par-la-Ville, Hamilton, Bermuda.

BORNEO: see INDONESIA, NORTH BORNEO and SARAWAK

BRAZIL
General
Some entries for bap 1788 and 1813-47, mar 1815-89 in 'International memoranda' at Guildhall Library: see page 6.

Bahia
Bap 1821, bur 1821-2: Guildhall Library, in Ms. 11,217 (index in Ms. 15,061/1-2).
Mar 1816-20: PRO Chancery Lane, in RG33/155 (index in RG43/7).

For addresses of repositories see page 2

For other sources which may relate to places on this page see 'How to use this guide' (page 1)

Maranhao
Mar 1844: PRO Chancery Lane, in RG33/155 (index in RG43/7).

Morre Velho
Mar 1851-67: St Catherine's House (index at PRO Chancery Lane, in RG43/7).

Para
Births and deaths 1840-1: PRO Chancery Lane, in RG33/155 (index to births in RG43/1, deaths in RG43/3).

Pernambuco
Bap, mar and bur 1838-44: Guildhall Library, in Ms. 11,217 (index in Ms. 15,061/1-2).

Rio de Janeiro
Mar 1809-18: PRO Chancery Lane, in RG33/155 (index in RG43/7).
Bap, mar and bur 1840-4: Guildhall Library, Ms. 11,216 (index in Ms. 15,061/1-2).
Births 1850-9: PRO Kew, FO743/11.

São Paulo
Births 1932, mar 1933: PRO Kew, FO863/1-2.

BRITISH GUIANA (GUYANA)
Colony of Demerara, Georgetown (Stabroek)
Bap 1798: Guildhall Library, in Ms. 11,569.

Colony of Essequibo
Bap 1821-8, mar 1827: United Society for the Propagation of the Gospel.

BULGARIA
Plovdiv (Philippopolis)
Births 1880-1922, deaths 1884-1900: PRO Kew, FO868/1-2.

For addresses of repositories see page 2

For other sources which may relate to places on this page see 'How to use this guide' (page 1)

Rustchuk (Ruse)
Births 1867-1908, deaths 1867-1903: PRO Kew, FO888/1-2.

Sofia
Births 1934-40: PRO Kew, FO864/1.

Varna
Births 1856-1939, deaths 1851-1929: PRO Kew, FO884/1-5.

BURMA: see INDIA

CANADA
General
All original church registers are held locally in Canada. Some are held by the National Archives of Canada, 395 Wellington Street, Ottawa K1A 0N3, Canada, but most are in the churches themselves or in local repositories.

Civil registration records do not begin until the 1860s in Nova Scotia and Ontario, and later in the other Canadian provinces. For further details (also for details about Canadian census records, etc.) see *Tracing your Ancestors in Canada* (Public Archives of Canada, 1966); re-printed in *Genealogists' Magazine* vol 15 no 8 (1966).

For records of emigration to Canada see page 11.

Transcripts exist of the following registers:

Bay of Quinte, Ontario
Mar 1836-8: Society of Genealogists.

Cape Sable, Nova Scotia
Index to bap, mar and bur 1799-1841: L. H. Smith, *Cape Sable Vital Records* . . . (Clearwater, Florida, 1976).

Ernestown, Ontario
Bap and mar 1787-1814: Society of Genealogists.

Halifax, Nova Scotia
Bap, mar and bur 1749-68: Society of Genealogists.

For addresses of repositories see page 2

For other sources which may relate to places on this page see 'How to use this guide' (page 1)

Hallowell, Ontario
Mar 1803-23: Society of Genealogists.

Kingston, Ontario
Bap, mar and bur 1785-1811: printed in A. H. Young, *The Parish Register of Kingston, Upper Canada* (Kingston, 1921) (not available at Guildhall Library).

Montreal
Bap, mar and bur 1706-1980: Society of Genealogists.

St Mary's Bay, Nova Scotia
Bap and mar 1769-74 and 1799-1801, bur 1801: L. H. Smith, *St Mary's Bay . . . Parish Registers* (Clearwater, Florida, 1983).

Salmon River, Nova Scotia
Index to bap, mar and bur 1849-1907: L. H. Smith, *Salmon River Vital Records . . .* (Clearwater, Florida, 1978).

Twillingate, Newfoundland
Bap 1816-23: United Society for the Propagation of the Gospel.
For registers held locally in Newfoundland see J. Bishop, 'Newfoundland Family Records', in *Genealogists' Magazine* vol 20 no 9 (1982).

Note. Assistance in tracing other church registers may be obtainable from local genealogical societies in Canada, whose addresses can be found in M. Keysor (ed.), *Meyer's Directory of Genealogical Societies in the U.S.A. and Canada* (Mount Airy, Maryland, 1984) (available in the United Kingdom at the Society of Genealogists, but not at Guildhall Library).

CANARY ISLANDS: see SPAIN

CAPE VERDE ISLANDS: see PORTUGAL

CEYLON (SRI LANKA)
Mar 1817 in 'International memoranda' at Guildhall Library: see page 6.

For addresses of repositories see page 2

For other sources which may relate to places on this page see 'How to use this guide' (page 1)

Enquiries about other records (from 1704) should be addressed to the Registrar General's Office, Colombo 1, Sri Lanka.

CHILE
Some entries for bap 1836-90, mar 1836-87 in 'International memoranda' at Guildhall Library: see page 6.

CHINA
General
Births, mar and deaths at various places in China 1850-1952: PRO Kew, FO387, FO564 and FO663-81.

Some entries for bap 1872-1907, mar 1864-1911 in 'International memoranda' at Guildhall Library: see page 6.

Chekiang
Bap 1903-1935, mar 1873 and 1903-49: Church Missionary Society.

Formosa: see *Taiwan*

Hong Kong
Deaths 1941-5: PRO Chancery Lane, RG33/11 (index in RG43/14).

Macao
Mar 1792 in 'International memoranda' at Guildhall Library: see page 6.

Births, mar and deaths 1819-28: printed in *East India Register* 1821-9.

Bap, mar and bur 1820-33: India Office Library, in N/9/1 (index in Z/N/9/1).

Bap 1820-38, mar 1822-38, bur 1821-38: Guildhall Library, in Ms. 11,218 (index in Ms. 15,061/1-2).

Shanghai
Bap 1849-1951, mar 1852-1947, bur 1859-99: Lambeth Palace Library, Mss. 1564-84.

Mar 1852-1951: PRO Chancery Lane, RG33/12-32 (index in RG43/7, 9-14).

For addresses of repositories see page 2

For other sources which may relate to places on this page see 'How to use this guide' (page 1)

Shantung
Bap 1906-50, mar 1912-48, bur 1934-46: Lambeth Palace Library, Mss. 1761-4.
Mar 1912-42: PRO Chancery Lane, RG33/33.

Szechwan: see *West China diocese*

Taiwan (Formosa)
Deaths 1873-1901: PRO Kew, FO721/1.

Weihaiwei
Births, mar and deaths 1899-1930: PRO Chancery Lane, RG33/34 (index in RG43/19).

West China diocese (Szechwan)
Bap 1895-1951: Guildhall Library, Ms. 17,360 (transcript 1895-1907, Ms. 11,218C; bap 1895-1907 also entered and indexed in 'International memoranda', for which see page 6).
Mar 1888-1948: Guildhall Library, Ms. 17,361 (mar 1889-1911 also entered and indexed in 'International memoranda', for which see page 6).
Mar 1894-1950: Guildhall Library, Mss. 11,218A-B (mar 1894-1911 also entered and indexed in 'International memoranda', for which see page 6; index to mar 1912-1950 in Ms. 15,061/1-2, under 'China').

Whampoa
Bur 1820-24: Guildhall Library, in Ms. 11,218 (index in Ms. 15,061/1-2).
Bur 1820-34: India Office Library, in N/9/1 (index in Z/N/9/1).

COLOMBIA

Mar 1824-7: PRO Chancery Lane, in RG33/155 (index in RG43/7).
Some entries for bap 1851, mar 1839-82 in 'International memoranda' at Guildhall Library: see page 6.
Births 1853-1924, deaths 1858-1927: PRO Kew, FO736/2-3.

CORSICA: see FRANCE

CUBA: see WEST INDIES

For addresses of repositories see page 2

For other sources which may relate to places on this page see 'How to use this guide' (page 1)

CURAÇAO
Births 1897-1966, mar 1922-9, deaths 1889-1965: PRO Kew, in FO907/1-32.

CYPRUS
Bap 1939-52: Society of Genealogists.

DENMARK
General

Many entries in 'Miscellaneous' series 1826-1951 at PRO Chancery Lane (see page 8); the series also includes separate death registers for Denmark and its colonies 1842-72 (RG35/4-7).

Some entries for bap 1816-33, mar 1826-89 in 'International memoranda' at Guildhall Library: see page 6.

Copenhagen

Bap 1836-65, mar 1835-65, bur 1836-65: Guildhall Library, Ms. 11,212 (index in Ms. 15,061/1-2).

Mar 1853-70: PRO Kew, FO211/236.

Mar 1853-74: PRO Chancery Lane, RG33/35 (index in RG43/7).

Elsinore

Bap 1833-8, bur 1833-9: Guildhall Library, Ms. 11,213 (index, 1833-5 only, in Ms. 15,061/1-2).

DOMINICA: see WEST INDIES

DOMINICAN REPUBLIC: see WEST INDIES

DUTCH EAST INDIES: see INDONESIA

DUTCH GUIANA: see SURINAM

ECUADOR
Guayaquil

Births, mar and deaths 1879-96: PRO Kew, FO521/2.

For addresses of repositories see page 2

For other sources which may relate to places on this page see 'How to use this guide' (page 1)

EGYPT

Alexandria

Bap, mar and bur 1841-59: Guildhall Library, Ms. 11,215 (index in Ms. 15,061/1-2).

Mar 1842 in 'International memoranda' at Guildhall Library: see page 6.

Church of Scotland bap 1858-1957, mar 1860-1954: National Library of Scotland, George IV Bridge, Edinburgh EH1 1EW.

Cairo

Church of Scotland bap 1899-1959, mar 1910-56: National Library of Scotland, George IV Bridge, Edinburgh EH1 1EW.

ESTONIA: see RUSSIA

FALKLAND ISLANDS

Port Stanley

Bap 1840-1949, mar 1844-1949, bur 1838-1949: Society of Genealogists.

FINLAND

Abo: see *Turku*

Brahestad: see *Raahe*

Helsinki

Births 1914-24, deaths 1924: PRO Kew, FO753/19 and FO768/5.

Bap 1920-47, mar 1921-61, banns 1926-50, bur 1921-38, cremations 1933-49: Guildhall Library, Ms. 20,892. Transcript of bap 1920-39 (incomplete), mar 1921-4 and 1926-39, bur 1921-38, cremations 1933-9: Ms. 11,214, indexed in Ms. 15,061/1-2. Duplicate register of bap 1946, mar 1941 and 1949-51: Ms. 20,892A.

Kristinestad

Deaths 1928: PRO Kew, FO756/1.

Raahe (Brahestad)

Deaths 1930: PRO Kew, FO755/1.

For addresses of repositories see page 2

For other sources which may relate to places on this page see 'How to use this guide' (page 1)

Tampere
Births 1906-23, deaths 1909-34: PRO Kew, FO769/1-2.

Turku (Abo)
Births 1928, deaths 1929: PRO Kew, FO754/1-2.

Vyborg: see *RUSSIA*

FORMOSA: see CHINA, Taiwan

FRANCE
General
Many entries in 'Miscellaneous' series 1826-1951 at PRO Chancery Lane (see page 8); the series also includes separate death registers for France and its colonies 1831-71 (RG35/8-16) and for France 1914-21 (military deaths only; incomplete) (RG35/45-57).
Some entries for bap 1817-1916, mar 1816-90, bur 1817-22 in 'International memoranda' at Guildhall Library: see page 6.

Aix les Bains
Bap 1886-1933, mar 1921-7, bur 1885-1938: Guildhall Library, Ms. 14,593.

Arras
Bap 1972-5: Guildhall Library, in Ms. 21,477.

Avranches
Bap 1821-8: Guildhall Library, in Ms. 10,891B (index in Ms. 15,061/1-2).
Bap 1828-1905, mar 1867-94, bur 1829-1908: United Society for the Propagation of the Gospel.
Bap and bur 1864-73: Guildhall Library, in Ms. 11,222 (index in Ms. 15,061/1-2).

Biarritz
Bap 1862-80, bur 1874-80: Guildhall Library, in Ms. 11,222 (index in Ms. 15,061/1-2).

For addresses of repositories see page 2

For other sources which may relate to places on this page see 'How to use this guide' (page 1)

Bur 1963-9: Guildhall Library, in Ms. 15,703A.

Boulogne
Bap 1815-96, mar 1829-95, bur 1815-96: PRO Chancery Lane, RG33/37-48 (index to bap in RG43/1, mar in RG43/7, bur in RG43/3).
Bap 1817-46, mar 1833-46, bur 1815-46: Guildhall Library, Ms. 10,891A (index in Ms. 15,061/1-2).
Bap, mar and bur 1847-1901: British Library, Add. Ms. 36,992.
Mar 1897-1940: Guildhall Library, Ms. 21,023.
Mar 1906-24: Guildhall Library, Ms. 21,024.
Bur 1972-3: Guildhall Library, in Ms. 21,477. Bur 1972 also in Ms. 16,944.

Brest
Births 1842: PRO Chancery Lane, in RG33/155 (index in RG43/1).

Calais
Bap 1817-78, mar 1818-72, bur 1819-78: PRO Chancery Lane, RG33/50-5 (index in RG33/49).
Bur 1858-1904: Guildhall Library, Ms. 21,025.
Bur 1972: Guildhall Library, in Ms. 16,944.

Cannes
Bap, mar and bur 1870-9: Guildhall Library, Ms. 20,987.

Corsica
Death 1879: Guildhall Library, in Ms. 20,996.

Dieppe
Bap 1825-9, bur 1825-8: Guildhall Library, in Ms. 10,891B (index in Ms. 15,061/1-2).
Births 1872-92, deaths 1871-94: PRO Kew, FO712/1-3.

La Rochelle
Bur 1831-5: Guildhall Library, in Ms. 11,818.

For addresses of repositories see page 2

For other sources which may relate to places on this page see 'How to use this guide' (page 1)

Le Havre
Bap, mar and bur 1817-63: PRO Chancery Lane, RG33/56-7 (index to bap in RG43/1, mar in RG43/7, bur in RG43/3).

Le Touquet
Bap 1968 and 1971: Guildhall Library, in Ms. 16,944.

Le Tréport
Births 1917-26, deaths 1899-1929: PRO Kew, FO713/1-2.

Lille
Bap 1859-63: Guildhall Library, in Ms. 11,222 (index in Ms. 15,061/1-2).

Lyons
Bap 1854-1967: Guildhall Library, in Ms. 14,533.
Mar 1868-1969: Guildhall Library, Ms. 14,534.
Banns 1878-1911: Guildhall Library, Ms. 14,535.
Bur 1863-1961: Guildhall Library, Ms. 14,536.

Monaco
Bap and bur 1892-1951: Society of Genealogists.

Nantes
Bap 1867-79: Guildhall Library, Ms. 11,222B.
Mar 1851-67: PRO Kew, FO384/1.

Nice
Bap 1823-38, mar 1826-38, bur 1822-38: Guildhall Library, in Ms. 11,222 (index in Ms. 15,061/1-2).
Bap and bur 1868-84: Guildhall Library, Ms. 20,988.

Paris
Bap 1784-9 and 1801-69, mar 1784-9 and 1801-90, bur 1784-9 and 1801-69: PRO Chancery Lane, RG33/58-77 (index to bap in RG43/1, mar in RG43/7, bur in RG43/3).
Bap 1816-28, mar 1816-45, bur 1815-28: Guildhall Library, Ms. 10,891 (index at front of Ms. 10,891 and in Ms. 15,061/1-2).

For addresses of repositories see page 2

For other sources which may relate to places on this page see 'How to use this guide' (page 1)

Bap 1830-2 and 1835-9, bur 1830-9: Guildhall Library, in Ms. 10,891B (index in Ms. 15,061/1-2, bap 1830-2 and bur 1830-5 under 'Germains', bap 1835-9 and bur 1836-9 under 'Paris').

Mar licence certificates and allegations 1828-9 and 1835-7: Guildhall Library, Ms. 10,891C.

Mar 1935-7: PRO Kew, FO630/1.

Pau

Bap 1842-4 and 1866-78, mar 1843-4 and 1868-77, bur 1865-78: Guildhall Library, in Ms. 11,222 (index to bap, mar and bur, to 1875 only, in Ms. 15,061/1-2).

Rennes

Mar 1826: Guildhall Library, in Ms. 10,891B (index in Ms. 15,061/1-2).

Rouen

Bap 1843-4: PRO Chancery Lane, RG33/78 (index in RG43/1).

Bap 1852-9: see *Sotteville-les-Rouen*.

St Malo

Bap 1838-42, bur 1838-9: Guildhall Library, in Ms. 10,891B (index in Ms. 15,061/1-2, under 'Malo').

St Omer

Bap 1817-47: PRO Chancery Lane, in RG33/50 (index in RG33/49).

St Servan

Bap and bur 1824-44: Guildhall Library, in Ms. 10,891B (index in Ms. 15,061/1-2).

Bap 1848-82, bur 1848-79: Guildhall Library, Ms. 11,222A/1 (index in Ms. 15,061/1-2).

Bap 1883-96, mar 1884-95, bur 1884-96: Guildhall Library, Ms. 11,222A/2 (index in Ms. 15,061/1-2).

Sotteville-les-Rouen

Bap 1852-9: Guildhall Library, in Ms. 11,222 (index in Ms. 15,061/1-2).

For addresses of repositories see page 2

For other sources which may relate to places on this page see 'How to use this guide' (page 1)

Tours
Bur 1841-3: Guildhall Library, in Ms. 11,818.

GERMANY
General
Some entries for bap 1819-91, mar 1817-91, deaths and bur 1858-92 in 'International memoranda' at Guildhall Library: see page 6.

Bap of civilians in chaplaincies of the British Army on the Rhine 1949-56: Guildhall Library, Ms. 11,225 (index in Ms. 15,061/1-2, under 'Germany').

Bap of civilians in chaplaincies of the British Army on the Rhine 1954-61: Guildhall Library, Ms. 11,225A (index in Ms. 15,061/1-2, under 'Germany').

Bap of civilians in chaplaincies of the British Army on the Rhine 1969-76: Guildhall Library, Ms. 11,225B.

Aachen (Aix la Chapelle)
Bap 1876-1918, mar 1919, bur 1898-1912: United Society for the Propagation of the Gospel.
Deaths 1925: PRO Kew, FO604/7.

Baden-Baden
Bap 1833-1928, mar 1838-1911, bur 1834-1923: United Society for the Propagation of the Gospel.
Bap 1833-92, mar 1838-90, bur 1834-91: Guildhall Library, Ms. 11,203 (index in Ms. 15,061/1-2).
Bap 1893-1912, mar 1894-1908, bur 1892-1908: Guildhall Library, Ms. 11,203A (index in Ms. 15,061/1-2).

Bavaria
Mar 1860-1 and 1884-97: PRO Kew, FO149/99 and FO151/3.

Berlin
Births 1944-54, deaths 1944-5: PRO Kew, FO601/2-6.

Bonn
Bap 1859-73, mar 1860 and 1873, bur 1859-73: Guildhall Library, Ms. 11,206 (index in Ms. 15,061/1-2).

For addresses of repositories see page 2

For other sources which may relate to places on this page see 'How to use this guide' (page 1)

Bremen
Births 1872-1914, mar 1893-1933: PRO Kew, FO585/1-5.

Bremerhaven
Births 1872-93, mar 1903-14: PRO Kew, FO585/1 and FO586/1.

Breslau: see POLAND

Cologne
Births and mar 1850-66, deaths 1850-66 and 1879-81: PRO Kew, FO155/5-11, 17.
Births 1880, mar 1920-34: PRO Kew, FO604/8-10.

Danzig: see POLAND

Darmstadt
Births 1869-98, deaths 1871-1905: PRO Kew, FO716/1-2.

Dresden
Births, bap and bur 1817-36: PRO Chancery Lane, RG33/79 (index to births and bap in RG43/1, bur in RG43/3).
Bap 1837-49, mar 1898, bur 1837-48: Guildhall Library, Ms. 11,205 (index to bap and bur in Ms. 15,061/1-2).
Births and deaths 1859-66: PRO Chancery Lane, RG33/80 (index to births in RG43/1, deaths in RG43/3).
Births 1901-7, mar 1899-1900: PRO Kew, FO292/2, 4-5.

Düsseldorf
Bap and bur 1861-77: Guildhall Library, Ms. 11,204 (index to bap and bur 1861-8 in Ms. 15,061/1-2).
Births 1873-84, bap 1903-7, mar 1873-8 and 1893-8, deaths 1876-84: PRO Kew, FO604/1-6, 8.

Essen
Births 1922-7: PRO Kew, FO604/11.

For addresses of repositories see page 2

For other sources which may relate to places on this page see 'How to use this guide' (page 1)

Frankfurt am Main
Mar 1836-65: PRO Kew, FO208/90.

Freiburg im Breisgau
Bap 1863-1914, mar 1903-6, bur 1863-1913: United Society for the Propagation of the Gospel.

Hamburg
Bap, mar and bur 1617-1807: Staatsarchiv of Hamburg, ABC-strasse 19, 2 Hamburg, Germany.
Bur 1665-1716: printed in *Genealogists' Magazine* vol 10 no 14 (1950).
Bap and mar 1820-38, bur 1821-38: Guildhall Library, Ms. 11,201 (index in Ms. 15,061/1-2).

Hanover
Bap, mar, deaths and bur 1839-59: PRO Chancery Lane, RG33/81 (index to bap in RG43/1, mar in RG43/7, deaths and bur in RG43/3).
Births 1861-6: PRO Kew, FO717/1.

Heidelberg
Bap 1869-1914, mar 1889: United Society for the Propagation of the Gospel.

Karlsruhe
Births 1860-4, deaths 1859-64: PRO Kew, FO718/1-2.

Konigsberg: see *RUSSIA*

Leipzig
Mar 1850-65, deaths 1850-69: PRO Kew, FO299/22.
Bap 1864-76, mar 1865-75, banns 1867-75, bur 1866-76: Guildhall Library, Ms. 11,205A (index in Ms. 15,061/1-2).

Munich
Bap 1862-7: Guildhall Library, Ms. 11,207 (index in Ms. 15,061/1-2).

Saxony
Mar 1850-65, deaths 1850-69: PRO Kew, FO218/3.

For addresses of repositories see page 2

For other sources which may relate to places on this page see 'How to use this guide' (page 1)

Silesia: see **POLAND**

Stettin: see **POLAND**

Wiesbaden

Bap 1848-67, mar 1865-6, bur 1848-66: Guildhall Library, Ms. 11,202/1 (index in Ms. 15,061/1-2).

Bap 1868-76, mar 1871-6, bur 1867-76: Guildhall Library, Ms. 11,202/2 (index in Ms. 15,061/1-2).

GIBRALTAR

Military bap and mar 1807-12, bur 1807: Guildhall Library, Ms. 10.446D (index in Ms. 15,061/1-2).

Military mar 1810 in 'International memoranda' at Guildhall Library: see page 6.

Mar allegations 1859-73: Guildhall Library, Ms. 20,979.

Other registers (civilian from 1696, military from 1769) are held locally in Gibraltar. See L. R. Burness, 'Genealogical Research in Gibraltar', in *Genealogists' Magazine* vol 21 no 1 (1983).

GREECE

General

Some entries for bap 1827-93, mar 1829-90 in 'International memoranda' at Guildhall Library: see page 6.

Athens

Bap 1834-1931, mar 1840-1945, bur 1840-1941: Society of Genealogists.

Ionian Islands

Births, bap and mar 1818-64, deaths and bur 1836-64: St Catherine's House (index at PRO Chancery Lane, births and bap in RG43/1, mar in RG43/7, deaths and bur in RG43/3).

Bap, mar, deaths and bur 1849-59: PRO Chancery Lane, RG33/82 (index to bap in RG43/1, mar in RG43/7, deaths and bur in RG43/3).

Bap 1874: Guildhall Library, in Ms. 20,996.

GRENADA: see WEST INDIES

For addresses of repositories see page 2

For other sources which may relate to places on this page see 'How to use this guide' (page 1)

GUADELOUPE: see WEST INDIES

GUATEMALA
Mar 1863 in 'International memoranda' at Guildhall Library: see page 6.

GUYANA: see BRITISH GUIANA

HAITI: see WEST INDIES

HAWAII
Honolulu
Births 1848-93: PRO Kew, FO331/59.
Mar 1850-3: PRO Chancery Lane, RG33/155 (index in RG43/7).

HOLLAND: see NETHERLANDS

HONG KONG: see CHINA

HUNGARY
Budapest
Mar 1872-99: PRO Kew, FO114/1-5.

INDIA
General
Bap, mar and bur, apparently complete for all India 1698-1948, and incomplete 1949-68: India Office Library, N/1-5 and N/10-11 (indexes in Z/N/1-5 and Z/N/10-11). These records include bap, mar and bur for former parts of India which are now Burma, Pakistan and Bangladesh.

For details of other biographical material at the India Office Library, see I. A. Baxter, *India Office Library and Records: A Brief Guide to Biographical Sources* (London, 1979).

Registers or transcripts for the following localities are available at repositories other than the India Office Library, and/or in published form:

For addresses of repositories see page 2

For other sources which may relate to places on this page see 'How to use this guide' (page 1)

Amritsar
Bap 1878-1946, mar 1853-1944: Society of Genealogists.

Assam
Church of Scotland bap, mar and bur 1939-59: Scottish Record Office, H.M. General Register House, Edinburgh EH1 3YY.

Bengal
Bap 1713-88, mar 1713-92, bur 1713-88: Society of Genealogists.
Births, mar and deaths 1807-43: printed in *East India Register* 1809-44.
Births, mar and deaths 1813-62: printed in *Bengal Directory* 1814-63 (only 1826 available at Guildhall Library).
Mar 1821 in 'International memoranda' at Guildhall Library: see page 6.

Bikaner: see *Indian Native States*

Bombay
Births, mar and deaths 1805-81: printed in *Bombay Directory* 1806-82 (not available at Guildhall Library).
Births, mar and deaths 1807-43: printed in *East India Register* 1809-44.
Bap 1818: Guildhall Library, in Ms. 11,219 (index in Ms. 15,061/1-2).

Burma, Rangoon
Mar 1929-42: PRO Chancery Lane, RG33/10 (index in RG43/11-13).

Dalhousie
Bap 1862-1935, mar 1865-1942: Society of Genealogists.

Deccan States: see *Kolhapur and Deccan States*

Delhi
Mar extracts 1861-1913: Society of Genealogists.

Gurdaspur
Bap and mar extracts 1871-1945: Society of Genealogists.

Gwalior: see *Indian Native States*

For addresses of repositories see page 2

For other sources which may relate to places on this page see 'How to use this guide' (page 1)

Hyderabad: see *Indian Native States*

Indian Native States
Births and deaths 1894-1947: PRO Chancery Lane, RG33/90-113 (index in RG43/15).

Jaipur: see *Indian Native States*

Jammu and Kashmir
Births 1917-47: PRO Chancery Lane, RG33/157.

Kalka
Bap 1901-43, mar 1921-42, bur 1883-1943: Society of Genealogists.

Kasauli
Bap, mar and bur extracts 1843-1945: Society of Genealogists.

Kashmir: see *Jammu and Kashmir*

Kolhapur and Deccan States
Births 1930-46: PRO Chancery Lane, RG33/158.

Madras
Mar 1680-1815: printed in *Marriages at Fort St George, Madras, 1680-1815* (anon.; Exeter, 1907) (not available at Guildhall Library); also in *The Genealogist*, New series, vol 19-23 (1903-7).

Bur 1680-1900: printed in C. H. Malden, *Burials at St Mary's, Madras, 1680-1900* (Madras, 1903-5) (not available at Guildhall Library).

Births, mar and deaths 1805-1903: printed in *Madras Almanac* 1806-1904 (only 1806 available at Guildhall Library).

Births, mar and deaths 1807-43: printed in *East India Register* 1809-44.

Church of Scotland bap 1842-1929: Society of Genealogists.

Madras States: see *Indian Native States*

Murree
Bap and bur 1853-1925: Society of Genealogists.

For addresses of repositories see page 2

For other sources which may relate to places on this page see 'How to use this guide' (page 1)

Mysore: see *Indian Native States*

Punjab States: see *Indian Native States*

Rajputana (Eastern): see *Indian Native States*

Rangoon: see *Burma*

Serampore
Baptist bap 1796-1822: Baptist Missionary Society.

Simla
Bap 1841-54, mar 1838-94, bur 1838-1945: Society of Genealogists.

Srinagar
Deaths 1926-47: PRO Chancery Lane, RG33/159.

Travancore: see *Indian Native States*

Trichinopoly
Bap 1751-1847, mar 1767-91 and 1805-42: United Society for the Propagation of the Gospel.

Trivandrum: see *Indian Native States*

Udaipur
Births 1938-47: PRO Chancery Lane, RG33/160.

INDONESIA (DUTCH EAST INDIES)
General
Many entries among registrations for the Netherlands and its colonies in 'Miscellaneous' series 1826-1951 at PRO Chancery Lane (see page 8).

Borneo, Balik Papan
Births 1907, deaths 1897-1907: PRO Kew, FO221/2-3.

Java, Semarang
Births 1869-1941, bap 1906, deaths 1874-98 and 1912-40: PRO Kew, FO803/1-3

For addresses of repositories see page 2

For other sources which may relate to places on this page see 'How to use this guide' (page 1)

Sumatra, Fort Marlborough
Bap, mar and bur 1759-1825: India Office Library, N/7/1 - 7/1).
Births, mar and deaths 1818-23: printed in *East India*

Sumatra, Oleh Leh (Ule Lue)
Births and deaths 1883-4: PRO Kew, FO220/12.

IONIAN ISLANDS: see GREECE

IRAN (PERSIA)
General
Births 1903-50, mar 1895-1950, deaths 1889-1950 at various places in Iran: PRO Kew, FO923/1-25.

Abadan
Mar 1913 in 'International memoranda' at Guildhall Library: see page 6.

Bushire
Births, bap, mar and deaths 1849-95: PRO Kew, FO560.

Isfahan
Births 1892-1950, mar 1893-1951, deaths 1892-1943: PRO Kew, FO799/34-7.

Julfa
Bap 1870-9, mar 1877, bur 1873 in 'International memoranda' at Guildhall Library: see page 6. Bap 1875-8 and mar 1877 also in Ms. 11,215A.

Tabriz
Bap 1844 in 'International memoranda' at Guildhall Library: see page 6.
Births 1851-1932, mar 1850-1923, deaths 1882-1931: PRO Kew, FO451/1-8.

For addresses of repositories see page 2

For other sources which may relate to places on this page see 'How to use this guide' (page 1)

1811-1969: Society of Genealogists.

IRAQ (MESOPOTAMIA)
General

Births, bap, mar and deaths 1915-31 at various places in Iraq: PRO Chancery Lane, RG33/133-7 (index in RG33/138-9 and RG43/16).

Bap 1916-22, mar 1917-28 at various places in Iraq: Lambeth Palace Library, Mss. 2669 and 2672.

Baghdad

Bap 1883-1967, mar 1922-46, bur 1922-41: Lambeth Palace Library, Mss. 2669-70, 2673 and 2676.

Basrah

Mar 1922-8: Guildhall Library, Ms. 11,221 (index in Ms. 15,061/1-2).

Bap 1943-56, mar 1943-66, bur 1943-53: Lambeth Palace Library, Mss. 2505, 2507 and 2675.

Kirkuk

Bap 1947-72, mar 1947-57: Lambeth Palace Library, Mss. 2671 and 2674.

ISRAEL: see PALESTINE

ITALY
General

Some entries for bap 1818-93, mar 1814-90, bur 1856-85 in 'International memoranda' at Guildhall Library: see page 6.

Florence

Bap, mar and bur 1833-51: Guildhall Library, Ms. 20,989/1. Bap 1835-6 also entered in Ms. 11,208 (and indexed in Ms. 15,061/1-2, under 'Rome').

For addresses of repositories see page 2

For other sources which may relate to places on this page see 'How to use this guide' (page 1)

Bap 1851-65, 1869, 1871-9, 1881-7 and 1899, mar 1852-65 and 1869, bur 1851-65 and 1869: Guildhall Library, Ms. 20,989/2.

Mar 1840-55 and 1865-71: PRO Chancery Lane, RG33/114-15 (index in RG43/7).

Mar 1856: PRO Kew, FO352/43.

Genoa

Bap 1824-49, mar 1825-49, bur 1824-49: Guildhall Library, Ms. 11,210 (index in Ms. 15,061/1-2).

Leghorn

Bap, mar and bur 1707-1824: PRO Chancery Lane, RG33/116-17 (index to bap in RG43/1, mar in RG43/7, bur in RG43/3).

Mar 1823: Guildhall Library, in Ms. 11,211 (index in Ms. 15,061/1-2).

Bap 1825-51, mar 1826-50, bur 1825-51: Guildhall Library, Ms. 20,990. Bap 1832-7, mar 1832-5 and bur 1832-7 also entered in Ms. 11,211 (and indexed in Ms. 15,061/1-2).

Naples

Bap, mar and bur 1817-22: PRO Chancery Lane, RG33/118 (index to bap in RG43/1, mar in RG43/7, bur in RG43/3).

Bap 1830-60, mar and bur 1831-60: Guildhall Library, Ms. 11,209 (index, except 1855, in Ms. 15,061/1-2).

Bap, mar and bur 1835-6: PRO Chancery Lane, in RG33/155 (index to bap in RG43/1, mar in RG43/7, bur in RG43/3).

Pegli

Bap 1875-1909, mar 1880, bur 1875-1971: United Society for the Propagation of the Gospel.

Pisa

Bap 1848: Guildhall Library, in Ms. 20,996.

Rome

Bap and mar 1816-52 (Rome and Tuscany): PRO Kew, FO170/6.

Bap and bur 1825-6: United Society for the Propagation of the Gospel.

Bap 1826-69, mar 1835-65, bur 1825-69: Guildhall Library, Ms. 11,208 (index in Ms. 15,061/1-2).

For addresses of repositories see page 2

For other sources which may relate to places on this page see 'How to use this guide' (page 1)

Bap, mar and bur 1875-7: Guildhall Library, Ms. 20,991.
Mar 1872-89: PRO Chancery Lane, RG33/119 (index in RG43/7).

San Remo
Bap 1867-76, bur 1865-75: Guildhall Library, Ms. 20,992.

Sicily
Births 1810-1957, deaths 1847-1957: PRO Kew, FO653/2-28 and FO720/1.
Bap 1838: PRO Chancery Lane, in RG33/155 (index in RG43/1).

Trieste
Bap 1828: Guildhall Library, in Ms. 11,226.
Mar 1835: Guildhall Library, in Ms. 11,219 (index in Ms. 15,061/1-2).
Bap 1861-5, mar 1862-4, bur 1862-5: Guildhall Library, Ms. 20,993.

Turin
Bap 1830 and 1836: Guildhall Library, in Ms. 11,219 (index in Ms. 15,061/1-2).
Mar 1858-64: PRO Chancery Lane, RG33/120 (index in RG43/7).
Bap and bur 1866-7: Guildhall Library, Ms. 11,830 (index in Ms. 15,061/1-2).

Tuscany: see *Rome;* see also *Florence, Leghorn* and *Pisa*

Venice
Bap 1856-79, mar 1874-9, bur 1871-9: Guildhall Library, Ms. 20,997.
Mar 1874-1947: PRO Chancery Lane, RG33/121 (index in RG43/7).

JAMAICA: see WEST INDIES

JAPAN
General
Some entries for mar 1867-90 in 'International memoranda' at Guildhall Library: see page 6.

For addresses of repositories see page 2

For other sources which may relate to places on this page see 'How to use this guide' (page 1)

Kobe
Bap 1874-1941, mar 1874-1940, bur 1902-41: PRO Chancery Lane, RG33/122-6 (index in RG43/1-3, 6-8, 10-14).

Nagasaki
Births 1864-1940, mar 1922-40, deaths 1859-1944: PRO Kew, FO796/236-8.

Osaka
Mar 1892-1904: PRO Chancery Lane, RG33/127-30.

Shimonoseki
Births 1903-21, mar 1906-22, deaths 1903-21: PRO Kew, FO797/48-50.

Tokyo
Mar 1875-87: PRO Kew, in FO345/34.

Yokohama
Mar 1870-4: PRO Kew, in FO345/34.

JAVA: see INDONESIA

KENYA
Births 1905-24: PRO Chancery Lane, in RG36 (index in RG43/18).

KUWAIT
Bur 1909-35: Society of Genealogists.
Births, mar and deaths 1937-61: India Office Library, N/12/1-16.

LATVIA: see RUSSIA

LEBANON
Beirut
Mar c.1859-1939: PRO Kew, FO616/5.

For addresses of repositories see page 2

For other sources which may relate to places on this page see 'How to use this guide' (page 1)

LIBYA
Tripoli
Bap 1819 in 'International memoranda' at Guildhall Library: see page 6.
Mar 1916 and 1931-40, deaths 1938-9: PRO Kew, FO161/4-7.

LITHUANIA: see RUSSIA

MACAO: see CHINA

MADAGASCAR (MALAGASY REPUBLIC)
Antananarivo: see *Tananarive*

Diego Suarez
Births 1907-21: PRO Kew, FO711/1.

Tamatave
Mar 1890 in 'International memoranda' at Guildhall Library: see page 6.
Mar 1891: Guildhall Library, in Ms. 20,996.
Deaths 1935-40: PRO Kew, FO714.

Tananarive (Antananarivo)
Births 1865-8: PRO Kew, FO710/1.
Mar 1876-83 in 'International memoranda' at Guildhall Library: see page 6.

MADEIRA: see PORTUGAL

MALAGASY REPUBLIC: see MADAGASCAR

MALAWI: see NYASALAND

MALAYA
Bap, mar and bur in the East India Company's establishment at Penang (Prince of Wales Island), Malacca and Singapore 1799-1829: India Office Library, N/8/1 (index in Z/N/8/1). Later bap, mar and bur to

---

For addresses of repositories see page 2

For other sources which may relate to places on this page see 'How to use this guide' (page 1)

c.1867 included in main series of Indian registers at India Office Library: see *INDIA*.

Births, mar and deaths in the East India Company's establishment at Penang (Prince of Wales Island), Malacca and Singapore 1807-32: printed in *East India Register* 1809-33 (generally under 'Prince of Wales Island').

Some entries for mar 1883-6 in 'International memoranda' at Guildhall Library: see page 6.

Births, mar and deaths 1915-c.1946: PRO Chancery Lane, in RG36 (index in RG43/18).

Births 1920-48: PRO Chancery Lane, RG33/131 (index in RG43/1).

Deaths 1941-5: PRO Chancery Lane, in RG33/132 (index in RG43/14).

MALAYSIA: see MALAYA, NORTH BORNEO and SARAWAK

MALTA

Most registers are held locally in Malta, but the following are available in the United Kingdom:

Bap 1801-9, mar 1801-18, bur 1801-4: Society of Genealogists.

Some entries for bap 1806-14, mar 1817 in 'International memoranda' at Guildhall Library: see page 6.

Mar 1801-92: Lambeth Palace Library, Mss. 1470-1.

Mar 1809-50: Society of Genealogists.

Mar 1904-36: PRO Kew, FO161/7.

Bur 1857-99: Society of Genealogists.

Military bap (Mediterranean fleet) 1933-8: Greater London Record Office.

MESOPOTAMIA: see IRAQ

MEXICO
Mexico City

Bur 1827-1926: PRO Kew, FO207/58.

Births and deaths 1854-67: PRO Kew, FO723/1-2.

For addresses of repositories see page 2

For other sources which may relate to places on this page see 'How to use this guide' (page 1)

Vera Cruz
Births, deaths and bur 1858-67: PRO Chancery Lane, RG33/140 (index to births in RG43/1, deaths and bur in RG43/3).

MINORCA: see SPAIN, Balearic Islands

MONACO: see FRANCE

MONTSERRAT: see WEST INDIES

MOROCCO
Daralbaida
Bap 1898 in 'International memoranda' at Guildhall Library: see page 6.

Tangier
Bap 1874: Guildhall Library, in Ms. 20,996.

NETHERLANDS (HOLLAND)
General
Many entries in 'Miscellaneous' series 1826-1951 at PRO Chancery Lane (see page 8); the series also includes a separate death register for the Netherlands and its colonies 1839-71 (RG35/17).

Some entries for mar 1819-89 in 'International memoranda' at Guildhall Library: see page 6.

Scottish military bap and mar 1708-83: printed in *Scottish History Society* 1st series vol 38 (1901).

The registers of most English churches in the Netherlands are held in the Municipal Archives of the town or city where the church was situated. The following are available in the United Kingdom:

Hague, The
Bap 1627-1821, births 1837-9 and 1859-94, mar 1627-1889, deaths 1859-1907: PRO Chancery Lane, RG33/83-8 (index to bap and births in RG43/1, mar in RG43/7, deaths in RG43/3).

Bap 1815-25: printed in *The Genealogist* New series vol 26 (1910).

For addresses of repositories see page 2

For other sources which may relate to places on this page see 'How to use this guide' (page 1)

Rotterdam

Index to mar 1576-1811: in *Family History* vol 13 (1985-6).

Bap and mar 1708-94: PRO Chancery Lane, RG33/89 (index to bap in RG43/1, mar in RG43/7).

Bap 1815-16, mar 1816, bur 1815-16: Guildhall Library, MS. 11,200 (index in Ms. 15,061/1-2).

NEVIS: see WEST INDIES

NEWFOUNDLAND: see CANADA

NEW ZEALAND

All original church registers are held locally in New Zealand.

Enquiries about civil registration records (from 1848) should be addressed to the Registrar General of Births, Deaths and Marriages, Lambton Quay, Wellington, New Zealand.

For records of emigration to New Zealand see page 11.

For New Zealand sources other than church registers see N. T. Hansen, *Guide to Genealogical Sources in Australia and New Zealand* (Melbourne, 1963). Assistance may also be obtainable from the New Zealand Society of Genealogists, P.O. Box 8795, Symonds Street, Auckland, New Zealand.

NORTH BORNEO (SABAH)

Births, mar and deaths 1923-c.1946: PRO Chancery Lane, in RG36 (index in RG43/18).

Deaths 1941-5: PRO Chancery Lane, in RG33/132 (index in RG43/14).

NORWAY

Bodo

Births 1888-90, deaths 1895: PRO Kew, FO724/1-2.

Christiania: see *Oslo*

Drammen

Deaths 1906: PRO Kew, FO532/2.

For addresses of repositories see page 2

For other sources which may relate to places on this page see 'How to use this guide' (page 1)

Kragero
Deaths 1895: PRO Kew, FO725/1.

Lofoten Islands
Births 1883-91: PRO Kew, FO726/1.

Oslo (Christiania)
Births 1850-1932, mar 1853-1936, deaths 1850-1930: PRO Kew, FO529/1-14.

Porsgrunn and Skien
Births 1885-91: PRO Kew, FO531/2.

NYASALAND (MALAWI)
Births 1904-c.1950: PRO Chancery Lane, in RG36 (partial index in RG43/18).

PAKISTAN: see INDIA

PALESTINE (ISRAEL)
General
Births and deaths 1920-35: PRO Chancery Lane, RG33/141 (index in RG43/17).

Births and deaths 1936-48: PRO Chancery Lane, in RG36 (partial index in RG43/18).

Haifa
Church of Scotland bap 1945-8, mar 1943-7: National Library of Scotland, George IV Bridge, Edinburgh EH1 1EW.

Jaffa
Births 1900-14: PRO Kew, FO734/1.

Church of Scotland mar 1936-51: National Library of Scotland, George IV Bridge, Edinburgh EH1 1EW.

Jerusalem
Births 1850-1921, deaths 1851-1914: PRO Kew, FO617/3-5.

Military bap 1939-47: PRO Kew, WO156/6.

For addresses of repositories see page 2

For other sources which may relate to places on this page see 'How to use this guide' (page 1)

Sarafand
Military bap 1940-6, banns 1944-7: PRO Kew, WO156/7-8.

PERSIA: see IRAN

PERU
Some entries for bap 1825-44, mar 1835-71 in 'International memoranda' at Guildhall Library: see page 6.
Births 1837-41, mar 1827 and 1836, deaths 1837-41: PRO Chancery Lane, in RG33/155 (index to births in RG43/1, mar in RG43/7, deaths in RG43/3).

PHILIPPINES
Bap 1872 in 'International memoranda' at Guildhall Library: see page 6.

PITCAIRN ISLAND
Births, mar and deaths 1790-1854: Society for Promoting Christian Knowledge. Printed by the Society as *The Pitcairn Island Register Book* (London, 1929) (not available at Guildhall Library).

POLAND
Breslau (Wroclaw)
Births 1929-38, deaths 1932-8: PRO Kew, FO715/1-2.

Danzig (Gdansk)
Bap and mar 1706-1811: Lambeth Palace Library, Ms. 1847.
Births 1851-1910, deaths 1850-1914: PRO Kew, FO634/16-18.

Gdansk: see *Danzig*

Lodz
Births 1925-39: PRO Kew, FO869/1.

Silesia
Bap 1888 in 'International memoranda' at Guildhall Library: see page 6.

For addresses of repositories see page 2

For other sources which may relate to places on this page see 'How to use this guide' (page 1)

Stettin
Births 1864-1939, deaths 1857-1933: PRO Kew, FO719/1-2.
Mar 1855 in 'International memoranda' at Guildhall Library: see page 6.

Warsaw
Bap, mar and bur 1858-61: Guildhall Library, Ms. 11,197A (index in Ms. 15,061/1-2).
Bap 1951-3: Guildhall Library, in Ms. 11,225.

Wroclaw: see *Breslau*

PORTUGAL

General
Some entries for bap 1811-48, mar 1812-90 in 'International memoranda' at Guildhall Library: see page 6.

Azores, Ponta Delgada
Births, bap, mar, deaths and bur 1807-66: PRO Kew, FO559/1.
Bap and mar 1827-49, bur 1827-48: Guildhall Library, in Ms. 10,446E (index in Ms. 15,061/1-2, under 'Ponta Delgada').
Bap, mar and bur 1835-7: PRO Chancery Lane, in RG33/155 (index to bap in RG43/1, mar in RG43/7, bur in RG43/3).

Cape Verde Islands
Mar 1894-1922: PRO Kew, FO767/6-7.

Funchal: see *Madeira*

Lisbon
Bap 1721-93, mar 1721-94, bur 1721-93: Guildhall Library, Ms. 10,446/1 (index in Ms. 10,446/5).
Bap, mar and bur 1794-1807: Guildhall Library, Ms. 10,446/4 (index to bap and mar to 1807 and bur to 1799 in Ms. 10,446/5).
Mar 1721-1807 and 1812-61: Society of Genealogists.
Mar 'at a distance from Lisbon' 1764, 1780-1 and 1797-9: Guildhall Library, Ms. 10,446/3 (index in Ms. 10,446/5).

For addresses of repositories see page 2

For other sources which may relate to places on this page see 'How to use this guide' (page 1)

Mar 1765-83: Guildhall Library, Ms. 10,446/2 (index in Ms. 10,446/5).

Mar 1822-59: St Catherine's House (index at PRO Chancery Lane, in RG43/7).

Mar 1859-76: PRO Kew, FO173/8.

Madeira, Funchal

Bap and bur 1848-51: Guildhall Library, Ms. 10,446F (index in Ms. 15,061/1-2, under 'Funchal').

Oporto

Bap 1717-89, mar 1716-97, bur 1716-25 and 1784-7: Guildhall Library, Ms. 10,446A (index in Ms. 15,061/1-2, under 'Portugal'); printed in C. Sellers, *Oporto Old and New* (London, 1899).

Bap 1778-1807, mar 1799-1804, bur 1788-1807: Guildhall Library, Ms. 10,446B/1 (index in Ms. 15,061/1-2, under 'Portugal').

Bap, mar and bur 1814-74: PRO Chancery Lane, RG33/142 (index to bap in RG43/1, mar in RG43/7, bur in RG43/3).

Bap 1814-32, mar 1814-31, bur 1814-32: Guildhall Library, Ms. 10,446B/2 (index in Ms. 15,061/1-2, under 'Portugal').

Bap 1832-65, mar 1833-64, bur 1832-65: Guildhall Library, Ms. 10,446B/3 (index in Ms. 15,061/1-2, under 'Portugal').

Bap, mar and bur 1833: PRO Chancery Lane, in RG33/155 (index to bap in RG43/1, mar in RG43/7, bur in RG43/3).

Bur 1876-1912: printed in *Miscellanea Genealogica et Heraldica* 5th series vol 1 (1916).

Bap, mar and bur 1878-98: Guildhall Library, Ms. 20,994.

Bap 1905-7, mar 1905-6, bur 1905-7: Guildhall Library, Ms. 10,446C (index in Ms. 15,061/1-2, under 'Portugal').

Ponta Delgada: see *Azores*

REUNION
Mar 1864-1921: PRO Kew, FO322/1-2.

ROUMANIA
Braila
Births 1922-30, deaths 1921-9: PRO Kew, FO727/1-2.

For addresses of repositories see page 2

For other sources which may relate to places on this page see 'How to use this guide' (page 1)

Bucharest
Births 1851-1931, bap 1858-1948, deaths 1854-1929: PRO Kew, FO625/2-4, 6.
Bap and bur 1879: Guildhall Library, in Ms. 20,996.
Mar 1880-3 in 'International memoranda' at Guildhall Library: see page 6.

Constanta (Kustendje)
Bap 1864: Guildhall Library, in Ms. 20,996.
Births 1866-73: PRO Kew, FO887/1.

Galatz
Bap 1864: Guildhall Library, in Ms. 20,996.
Mar 1891-1939: PRO Kew, FO517/1-2.

Kustendje: see *Constanta*

Lower Danube
Bap 1869-1907: PRO Kew, FO625/5.
Mar 1868-1914: PRO Chancery Lane, RG33/143 (index in RG43/7).
Bur 1869-70: PRO Kew, FO786/120.

Sulina
Births 1861-1932, deaths 1860-1931: PRO Kew, FO728/1-2 and FO886/1-2.

RUSSIA (SOVIET UNION)
General
Many entries in 'Miscellaneous' series 1826-1951 at PRO Chancery Lane (see page 8); the series also includes separate registers of births, mar and deaths for Russia 1835-70 (RG35/18-19).

Some entries for bap 1926-37 in Helsinki registers at Guildhall Library: see under *FINLAND*.

Archangel
Bap and bur 1719: Guildhall Library, Ms. 11,192B.
Mar 1819: Guildhall Library, Ms. 11,195C.

For addresses of repositories see page 2

For other sources which may relate to places on this page see 'How to use this guide' (page 1)

Bap 1833-83, mar 1834-74, bur 1833-5 and 1879: Guildhall Library, Ms. 11,195 (index in Ms. 15,061/1-2).

Bur 1835-76: Guildhall Library, Ms. 11,195A (index in Ms. 15,061/1-2). Bur 1866 also in Ms. 11,195C.

Births 1849-1909, mar 1849-61, deaths 1849-1915: PRO Kew, FO267/44-6.

Bap 1915-18, mar 1915-19, bur 1913-19: Guildhall Library, in Ms. 11,195C. Transcript: Ms. 11,195B (index in Ms. 15,061/1-2).

Batum

Births 1884-1921, mar 1891-1920, deaths 1884-1920: PRO Kew, FO397/1-6.

Berdiansk (Osipenko)

Mar 1901: PRO Kew, FO399/1.

Cronstadt (Kronstadt)

Bap, mar and bur 1807-49: Guildhall Library, Ms. 11,196/1 (index in Ms. 15,061/1-2).

Bap 1850-94, mar 1850-87, bur 1850-94: Guildhall Library, Ms. 11,196/2 (index in Ms. 15,061/1-2).

Ekaterinburg (Sverdlovsk)

Deaths 1918-19: PRO Kew, FO399/5.

Estonia

Some entries for bap 1922-37, mar 1924-30, banns 1926-30, bur 1926-33 in Helsinki registers at Guildhall Library: see under *FINLAND*.

Estonia, Pernau

Births 1894-1930, deaths 1894-1933: PRO Kew, FO399/11-12.

Estonia, Tallinn (Reval)

Births 1866-1940, mar 1921-39, deaths 1875-1940: PRO Kew, FO514/1-9.

Feodosiya: see *Theodosia*

Kaliningrad: see *Konigsberg*

For addresses of repositories see page 2

For other sources which may relate to places on this page see 'How to use this guide' (page 1)

Konigsberg (Kaliningrad)
Births 1869-1933, mar 1864-1904, deaths 1857-1932: PRO Kew, FO509/1-4.

Kovno: see *Lithuania*

Kronstadt: see *Cronstadt*

Latvia, Libau
Births 1883-1932, deaths 1871-1932: PRO Kew, FO440/10 and FO661/4-5.
Bap 1893-1928: Guildhall Library, Ms. 10,953C/1.
Mar 1892-1905: Guildhall Library, Ms 10,953C/2. Duplicate: Ms. 10,953C/3.
Banns 1896-1911: Guildhall Library, Ms. 10,953C/4.
Bur 1898-1915: Guildhall Library, Ms. 10,953C/5.

Latvia, Riga
Bap 1830-1938: Guildhall Library, Ms. 10,953. Bap 1921-2 also in Ms. 10,953B/1 (index to bap 1921-2 in Ms. 15,061/1-2).
Mar 1831-1937: Guildhall Library, Ms. 10,953A. Mar 1921 also in Ms. 10,953B/1 (index to mar 1921 in Ms. 15,061/1-2).
Bur 1830-1939: Guildhall Library, Ms. 10,953B/2.
Births 1850-1910, deaths 1850-1915: PRO Kew, FO377/3-4.
Births 1921-40, mar 1920-40, deaths 1921-40: PRO Kew, FO516/1-9.

Latvia, Windau
Births 1906-9: PRO Kew, FO399/19.

Leningrad: see *St Petersburg*
Libau: see *Latvia*
Lithuania, Kovno and Memel
Births 1924-40, deaths 1922-40: PRO Kew, FO722/1-4.

Memel: see *Lithuania*

Moscow
Bap, mar and bur 1706-23: Guildhall Library, in Ms. 11,192B (with

---

For addresses of repositories see page 2

For other sources which may relate to places on this page see 'How to use this guide' (page 1)

index at back; also indexed in Ms. 15,061/1-2, under 'Petersburg').

Bap, mar and bur 1825-1920: Guildhall Library, as follows:

Registers: bap, mar and bur 1825-61: Ms. 11,192C
bap, mar and bur 1861-80: Ms. 11,192A
bap 1880-1920: Ms. 11,192/1
mar 1880-1920: Ms. 11,192/2
bur 1880-1920: Ms. 11,192/3

Transcripts (all indexed in Ms. 15,061/1-2):
bap 1825-64, mar 1826-64, bur 1825-64: Ms. 11,193/1
bap, mar and bur 1865-83: Ms. 11,193/2 part I
bap, mar and bur 1884-96: Ms. 11,193/2 part II
bap, mar and bur 1897-1907: Ms. 11,193/3 part I
bap, mar and bur 1908-19: Ms. 11,193/3 part II.

Mar 1826-58: St Catherine's House (index at PRO Chancery Lane, in RG43/7).

Births 1882-1918, mar 1894-1924, deaths 1881-1918: PRO Kew, FO518/1-4.

Nicolayev

Births 1872-1917, deaths 1874-1915: PRO Kew, FO399/7-8.

Novorossisk

Births 1911-20, deaths 1896-1920: PRO Kew, FO399/9-10.

Odessa

Bap 1818, mar 1821 in 'International memoranda' at Guildhall Library: see page 6.

Births 1852-1919, bap 1893, mar 1851-1916, deaths 1852-1919: PRO Kew, FO359/3-12.

Bap 1883-1908, mar 1884-91: Guildhall Library, Ms. 11,197/1.

Bap 1892-1918, mar 1892-1917: Guildhall Library, Ms. 11,197/2.

Banns 1905-17: Guildhall Library, Ms. 11,197/3.

Bur 1883-1901: Guildhall Library, Ms. 11,197/4.

Bur 1906-18: Guildhall Library, Ms. 11,197/5.

Osipenko: see *Berdiansk*

Pernau: see *Estonia*

For addresses of repositories see page 2

For other sources which may relate to places on this page see 'How to use this guide' (page 1)

Petrograd: see *St Petersburg*

Poti
Births 1871-1906, deaths 1871-1920: PRO Kew, FO399/13-14.

Reval: see *Estonia*

Riga: see *Latvia*

Rostov
Births 1891-1914, mar 1904-18, deaths 1906-16: PRO Kew, FO398/1-9.

St Petersburg (Petrograd, Leningrad)
Bap, mar and bur 1723-7 and 1737-1815: Guildhall Library, in Ms. 11,192B (index at back; also indexed in Ms. 15,061/1-2, under 'Petersburg').

Bap, mar and bur 1816-1918: Guildhall Library, as follows (all indexed in Ms. 15,061/1-2, under 'Petersburg'):

1816-28: Ms. 11,194/1 part I	1882-6: Ms. 11,194/3 part III
1830-9: Ms. 11,194/1 part II	1887-93 and 1895:
1840-9: Ms. 11,194/1 part III	Ms. 11,194/3 part IV
1850-6: Ms. 11,194/2 part I	1894 and 1896-1901:
1857-62: Ms. 11,194/2 part II	Ms. 11,194/4 part I
1863-7: Ms. 11,194/2 part III	1902-12: Ms. 11,194/4 part II
1868-77: Ms. 11,194/3 part I	1912-18: Ms. 11,194/4 part III.
1878-81: Ms. 11,194/3 part II	

Independent church bap 1818-40, bur 1821-40: PRO Chancery Lane, RG4/4605 (index to bap in RG43/1, bur in RG43/3).

Births, bap, mar, deaths and bur 1840-1918: PRO Chancery Lane, RG33/144-52 (index to births and bap in RG43/1, mar in RG43/7, deaths and bur in RG43/3).

Births 1856-1938, mar 1892-1917, deaths 1897-1927: PRO Kew, FO378/3-9.

Sebastopol
Births 1886-98, mar 1910, deaths 1893-1908: PRO Kew, FO399/3, 15-16.

Sverdlovsk: see *Ekaterinburg*

For addresses of repositories see page 2

For other sources which may relate to places on this page see 'How to use this guide' (page 1)

Tallinn: see *Estonia*

Theodosia (Feodosiya)
Births 1904-6, deaths 1907-18: PRO Kew, FO399/17-18.

Vladivostok
Births 1911-27, mar 1916-23, deaths 1908-24: PRO Kew, FO510/1-10.

Vyborg
Births 1924-31, deaths 1929-37: PRO Kew, FO757/1-3.

Windau: see *Latvia*

SABAH: see NORTH BORNEO

ST CHRISTOPHER: see WEST INDIES

ST HELENA
Bap, mar and bur 1767-1835: India Office Library, N/6/1-3 (index in Z/N/6/1).

ST KITTS: see WEST INDIES, St Christopher

ST LUCIA: see WEST INDIES

ST VINCENT: see WEST INDIES

SAMOA
Bap 1877 in 'International memoranda' at Guildhall Library: see page 6.

SARAWAK
Bap 1848-1950, births 1910-49, mar 1844-1953: Society of Genealogists.
Bap, mar and bur 1848-52: Guildhall Library, Ms. 11,220 (index in Ms. 15,061/1-2).
Births, mar and deaths 1910-c.1946: PRO Chancery Lane, in RG36 (index in RG43/18).
Deaths 1941-5: PRO Chancery Lane, in RG33/132 (index in RG43/14).

For addresses of repositories see page 2

For other sources which may relate to places on this page see 'How to use this guide' (page 1)

SICILY: see **ITALY**

SINGAPORE: see **MALAYA**

SOMALILAND (SOMALIA)
Births 1905-20: PRO Chancery Lane, in RG36 (index in RG43/18).

SOUTH AFRICA
General

A very few registers or register transcripts are available in the United Kingdom (see below), but almost all original church registers are held locally in South Africa.

For biographical details of early British settlers (before c.1826) see E. Morse Jones, *Roll of the British settlers in South Africa* (Capetown, 1971). See also P. Philip, *British residents at the Cape 1795-1819* (Capetown, 1981).

Enquiries about civil registration records (from 1838, but incomplete until early 20th century) should be addressed to the Registrar of Births, Marriages and Deaths, Dept. of the Interior, Private Bag XII4, Pretoria 0001, South Africa. Some further records of births 1842-96 and mar 1820-99 are held by the Central Archives Depot, Private Bag X236, Pretoria 0001, South Africa.

British military deaths in the Boer War 1899-1902 are registered at St Catherine's House.

For records of emigration to South Africa see page 11.

For further information about South African sources see R. J. T. Lombard, *Handbook for Genealogical Research in South Africa* (Pretoria, 1984) (not available at Guildhall Library).

Cape of Good Hope

Military bap 1795-1803, mar 1796-1803, bur 1795-1803: Guildhall Library, Ms. 11,569 (index in Ms. 15,061/1-2).

Deaths 1796-1826: extracts printed in *The Genealogist* New series vol 29 (1913) and vol 32 (1916).

Bap 1810-21, mar 1806-21: extracts printed in *The Genealogist* New series vol 30 (1914).

For addresses of repositories see page 2

For other sources which may relate to places on this page see 'How to use this guide' (page 1)

Grahamstown
Baptist bap and mar 1853-60: Society of Genealogists.

Port Elizabeth
Bap, mar and bur 1858-98: Society of Genealogists.

Simonstown
Mar 1862 in 'International memoranda' at Guildhall Library: see page 6.

Zululand, Melmoth
Bap 1896-1982: Society of Genealogists.

SOUTH GEORGIA
Bap, mar and bur 1910-48: Society of Genealogists.

SOUTH YEMEN: see ADEN

SOVIET UNION: see RUSSIA

SPAIN
General
Some entries for bap 1813-95, mar 1835-88 in 'International memoranda' at Guildhall Library: see page 6.

Aguilas
Births 1875-1911, deaths 1874-1911: PRO Kew, FO920/1-2.

Balearic islands, Minorca
Mar 1801 in 'International memoranda' at Guildhall Library: see page 6.

Bilbao
Deaths 1855-70: PRO Kew, FO729/1.

Canary islands, Las Palmas
Mar 1834: Guildhall Library, Ms. 11,219 (index in Ms. 15,061/1-2, under 'Grand Canary').

For addresses of repositories see page 2

For other sources which may relate to places on this page see 'How to use this guide' (page 1)

Cartagena
Births 1847-87, mar 1858-1904, deaths 1855-71: PRO Kew, FO920/3-6.

Garrucha
Births 1876-90, deaths 1883-1905: PRO Kew, FO920/7-8.

Jerez de la Frontera
Bap 1878-1966: Guildhall Library, Ms. 21,026.
Bur 1873-1977: Guildhall Library, Ms. 21,027.

Las Palmas: see *Canary islands*

Malaga
Bap and bur 1851-2: Guildhall Library, Ms. 20,995.

Minorca: see *Balearic islands*

Portman
Births 1907, deaths 1911: PRO Kew, FO920/9-10.

Seville
Bap 1865-79 and 1934, mar 1865-73 and 1930, bur 1865-79 and 1930: Guildhall Library, Ms. 21,028/1.
Bap 1880-4, bur 1880-91: Guildhall Library, Ms. 21,028/2.
Bap 1884-95, bur 1891-6: Guildhall Library, Ms. 21,028/3.
Bap 1896-1931 and 1936, mar 1910-28, bur 1899-1929 and 1931-6: Guildhall Library, Ms. 21,028/4.
Bap 1956-76, bur 1952-78: Guildhall Library, in Ms. 21,029.

SRI LANKA: see CEYLON

SUDAN
General
Births, mar and deaths 1906-c.1950: PRO Chancery Lane, in RG36 (partial index in RG43/18).

For addresses of repositories see page 2

For other sources which may relate to places on this page see 'How to use this guide' (page 1)

Atbara
Bap 1938-53, mar 1937-52: Lambeth Palace Library, Mss. 2782A-4.

Khartoum
Bap 1902-59, mar 1936-63, bur 1915-36: Lambeth Palace Library, Mss. 2660-3.

SUMATRA: see INDONESIA

SURINAM (DUTCH GUIANA)
Paramaribo
Births 1897-1966, mar 1922-9, deaths 1889-1965: PRO Kew, in FO907/1-32.

SWEDEN
General
Some entries for bap 1820-57, mar 1845-82 in 'International memoranda' at Guildhall Library: see page 6.

Gothenburg
Bap 1881-90: PRO Kew, FO818/15.
Mar 1845-91: PRO Chancery Lane, RG33/153 (index in RG43/7).

Hudiksvall
Deaths 1884: PRO Kew, FO730/1.

Oskarshamn
Deaths 1887: PRO Kew, FO731/1.

Stockholm
Births, mar and deaths 1920-38: PRO Kew, FO748.

SWITZERLAND
General
Some entries for bap 1820-1924, mar 1816-90, bur 1869-91 in 'International memoranda' at Guildhall Library: see page 6.
Mar at various places in Switzerland 1816-33: PRO Kew, FO194/1.

For addresses of repositories see page 2

For other sources which may relate to places on this page see 'How to use this guide' (page 1)

Berne

Bap 1832: Guildhall Library, in Ms. 10,926B (index in Ms. 15,061/1-2, under 'Geneva').

Chateau d'Oex

Bur 1871 and 1889-1946: Society of Genealogists.

Davos

Bap 1928-69: Guildhall Library, Ms. 21,661.
Mar 1910-28: Guildhall Library, Ms. 21,662.
Bur 1890-1913: Guildhall Library, Ms. 21,663.

Geneva

Bap and mar 1556-8, bur 1556-60: printed in J. S. Burn, *Livre des Anglois à Genève* (London, 1831).

Bap 1817-29, mar 1818-29, bur 1817-29: Guildhall Library, Ms. 10,926A/1 (index in Ms. 15,061/1-2).

Bap 1835-42, mar 1837-41, bur 1835-42: Guildhall Library, Ms. 10,926A/2 (index in Ms. 15,061/1-2). Bap 1835 also in Ms. 10,926B.

Births 1850-1934, mar 1850-1933, deaths 1850-1923: PRO Kew, FO778/13-22.

Lausanne

Bap 1828 and 1841: Guildhall Library, in Ms. 10,926B (index in Ms. 15,061/1-2, under 'Geneva').

Births 1886-1948, mar 1887-1947, deaths 1887-1948: PRO Kew, FO910/1-20.

Leysin

Bap 1917-18 and 1921: Guildhall Library, in Ms. 16,945/2.
Bap 1928, deaths 1927-31: Guildhall Library, in Ms. 16,945/3.
Bap 1940: Guildhall Library, in Ms. 16,945/4.
Mar 1914: Guildhall Library, in Ms. 16,945/1.

Lucerne

Bap 1864-8, bur 1863-8: Guildhall Library, in Ms. 10,926B (index in Ms. 15,061/1-2).

For addresses of repositories see page 2

For other sources which may relate to places on this page see 'How to use this guide' (page 1)

Bap 1868-1946, 1954 and 1957-65, bur 1868-1961 (including bur at the English cemetery at Meggen): Guildhall Library, Ms. 21,330. Bap 1884-1905 and bur 1885-1910 also in Ms. 21,473.

Bap 1864-1922, bur 1863-1921 (including bur at the English cemetery at Meggen): Guildhall Library, Ms. 21,331.

Bap 1932 and 1951-74: Guildhall Library, Ms. 21,475.

Mar 1884-1920: Guildhall Library, Ms. 21,332.

Mar 1893-1927: Guildhall Library, in Ms. 21,473.

Mar 1913-73: Guildhall Library, Ms. 21,474.

Meggen: see *Lucerne*

Montreux
Births 1902-39, mar 1927-33, deaths 1903-41: PRO Kew, FO911/1-3.

Nyon
Bap 1834-9: Guildhall Library, in Ms.10,926B (index in Ms. 15,061/1-2, under 'Geneva'). Bap 1835-7 also in Ms. 10,926A/2.

SYRIA
Aleppo
Bap, mar and bur 1756-1800: PRO Chancery Lane, SP110/70. Transcript at Society of Genealogists. Bap, mar and bur 1756-81 also printed in *The Pedigree Register* vol 3 (1914-15).

Damascus
Bap 1845 in 'International memoranda' at Guildhall Library: see page 6. Births, mar and deaths c.1932-8: PRO Kew, FO684.

TAHITI
Papeete
Births 1818-1941, mar 1845-1941, deaths 1845-1936: PRO Kew, FO687/23-33.

TAIWAN: see CHINA

For addresses of repositories see page 2

For other sources which may relate to places on this page see 'How to use this guide' (page 1)

TOBAGO: see **WEST INDIES**

TRINIDAD: see **WEST INDIES**

TRISTAN DA CUNHA
Mar 1871-1951, deaths 1892-1949: PRO Kew, PRO30/65.

TUNISIA
Births 1885-8, deaths 1894-1931: PRO Kew, FO870-5 and FO878/1-2.

TURKEY
General
Some entries for bap 1823-8, mar 1821-90 in 'International memoranda' at Guildhall Library: see page 6.

Adana
Mar 1913, 1942 and 1946: PRO Kew, FO609/1-3.

Adrianople (Edirne)
Births 1888-1912, mar 1887-1914: PRO Kew, FO783/3-7.

Ankara and Konya
Births 1895-1909: PRO Kew, FO732/1.

Constantinople (Istanbul)
Bap, mar and bur 1835-6: Guildhall Library, in Ms. 10,446E (index in Ms. 15,061/1-2).

Bap 1859-74: Church Missionary Society.

Bap 1860-4, 1868 and 1878, mar 1860-2, bur 1868: Guildhall Library, Ms. 20,998.

Mar 1885-1958: PRO Chancery Lane, RG33/154 (index in RG43/7, 11-12).

Mar 1895-1924: PRO Kew, FO441/1-35.

Mar 1909: Guildhall Library, in Ms. 11,827.

Dardanelles
Births 1900-14: PRO Kew, FO733/1.

For addresses of repositories see page 2

For other sources which may relate to places on this page see 'How to use this guide' (page 1)

Edirne: see *Adrianople*

Istanbul: see *Constantinople*

Izmir: see *Smyrna*

Konya: see *Ankara and Konya*

Smyrna (Izmir)
Bap 1795-1832, mar 1785 and 1797-1832, bur 1801-32: Guildhall Library, Ms. 10,446G (index in Ms. 15,061/1-2). Transcript at Society of Genealogists.
Bap, mar and bur 1833-49: PRO Chancery Lane, in RG33/155 (index to bap in RG43/1, mar in RG43/7, bur in RG43/3).

Note. For other places in the former Turkish empire see *BULGARIA, IRAQ, LEBANON, PALESTINE, ROUMANIA* and *SYRIA*.

UGANDA
Mar 1898 in 'International memoranda' at Guildhall Library: see page 6.
Births, mar and deaths 1905-18: PRO Chancery Lane, in RG36 (index in RG43/18).
Bap and mar 1921-63: Society of Genealogists.

UNITED STATES OF AMERICA
General
All original church registers are held locally in the United States, either in the churches themselves or in local repositories.

Civil registration records begin in the 1840s in a few American states, but in most states they do not begin until the late 19th or early 20th century. Details of these records, and addresses of state registration authorities, are given in G. B. Everton, *The Handy Book for Genealogists* (Logan, Utah, 1981) (not available at Guildhall Library).

For records of emigration to America see page 11.

For further information about American sources see G. H. Doane, *Searching for your Ancestors* (Minneapolis, 1973) (this book includes some details of the availability of civil registration records but does not give the location of individual church registers).

For addresses of repositories see page 2

For other sources which may relate to places on this page see 'How to use this guide' (page 1)

Aberdeen, British Consulate
Births 1916, deaths 1914: PRO Kew, FO700/22-3.

Barnstable
Births, mar and deaths 1642-1807: L. H. Smith, *Vital Records of Southeastern Massachusetts* vol 3 (Clearwater, Florida, 1982).

Boston, British Consulate
Births 1871-1932, deaths 1902-30: PRO Kew, FO706/1-3.

Dallas, British Consulate
Births 1951-4, deaths 1951: PRO Kew, FO700/24-5.

Eastham and Orleans
Births, mar and deaths 1643-1842: L. H. Smith, *Vital Records of Southeastern Massachusetts* vol 1 (Clearwater, Florida, 1980).

El Paso, British Consulate
Births 1916-30, deaths 1914-26: PRO Kew, FO700/26-7.

Galveston, British Consulate
Births 1838-1918, deaths 1850-1927: PRO Kew, FO701/23-4.

Honolulu: see *HAWAII*

Maryland
Mar 1634-1777: printed in R. Barnes, *Maryland Marriages* (Baltimore, 1975).

Middleborough
Births, mar and deaths 1666-1807: L. H. Smith, *Vital Records of Southeastern Massachusetts* vol 2 (Clearwater, Florida, 1981).

New Orleans, British Consulate
Births 1850-1932, mar 1852-81, deaths 1850-1932: PRO Kew, FO581/15 19.

For addresses of repositories see page 2

For other sources which may relate to places on this page see 'How to use this guide' (page 1)

Pensacola, British Consulate
Births 1880-1901, deaths 1879-1905: PRO Kew, FO885/1-2.

Portland, British Consulate
Births 1880-1926, deaths 1929: PRO Kew, FO707/1-2

Providence, British Consulate
Births 1902-30, deaths 1930: PRO Kew, FO700/8-9.

Sandwich
Births, mar and deaths 1636-1775: L. H. Smith, *Vital Records of Southeastern Massachusetts* vol 3 (Clearwater, Florida, 1982).

Tacoma, British Consulate
Births 1896-1921, deaths 1892-1907: PRO Kew, FO700/20-1.

Wareham
Births, bap, mar and deaths 1739-c.1891: L. H. Smith, *Records of the First Church of Wareham . . .* (Clearwater, Florida, 1974) and *Vital Records of Southeastern Massachusetts* vol 2 (Clearwater, Florida, 1981).

Washington, British Legation
Mar 1828 in 'International memoranda' at Guildhall Library: see page 6.

Note. Assistance in tracing other registers may be obtainable from local genealogical societies in the United States, whose addresses can be found in M. Keysor (ed.), *Meyer's Directory of Genealogical Societies in the U.S.A. and Canada* (Mount Airy, Maryland, 1984) (available in the United Kingdom at the Society of Genealogists, but not at Guildhall Library). Microfilm copies of many genealogical records are held by the Genealogical Society of the Church of Latter-Day Saints, 50 East North Temple Street, Salt Lake City, Utah 84150.

URUGUAY
Fray Bentos
Mar 1871-92: Guildhall Library, Ms. 11,223.

For addresses of repositories see page 2

For other sources which may relate to places on this page see 'How to use this guide' (page 1)

Montevideo
Bap 1843, mar 1881-90 in 'International memoranda' at Guildhall Library: see page 6.

VENEZUELA
Bap 1843-7, births 1850, deaths 1817, bur 1843 in 'International memoranda' at Guildhall Library: see page 6.
Mar 1836-8: PRO Chancery Lane, in RG33/155 (index in RG43/7).

VIRGIN ISLANDS: see WEST INDIES

WEST INDIES
General
Some register transcripts of former British colonies in the West Indian islands are available in the United Kingdom (see below), but all original church registers are held locally in the West Indies.
For records of emigration to the West Indies see page 11.

Anguilla
For registers (from 1826) held locally see E. C. Baker, *A Guide to Records in the Leeward Islands* (Oxford, 1965).

Antigua
Bap 1733-4 and 1738-45, mar 1745, bur 1733-4 and 1738-45: PRO Kew, in CO152/21,25; printed in *Caribbeana* vol 1 (1910).
Bap 1770-1830, mar 1710-1841, bur 1691-1839: extracts printed in *Miscellanea Genealogica et Heraldica* 2nd series vol 4 (1892).
For registers (from 1689) held locally see E. C. Baker, *A Guide to Records in the Leeward Islands* (Oxford, 1965).

Bahamas
Bap 1721-8, mar and bur 1723-8: Lambeth Palace Library, in Fulham Papers vol 15. Microfilm copy available at Guildhall Library, Microfilm 372.
Bap 1813-16, mar 1811 in 'International memoranda' at Guildhall Library: see page 6.

For addresses of repositories see page 2

For other sources which may relate to places on this page see 'How to use this guide' (page 1)

For registers (from 1744) held locally see D. G. Saunders and E. A. Carson, *Guide to the Records of the Bahamas* (Nassau, Bahamas, 1973).

Barbados

Mar 1643-1800: printed in J. McRee Sanders, *Barbados Records* (Houston, Texas, 1982).

Mar 1643-1700: British Library, Add. Ms. 38,825.

Mar 1648-52: printed in *Caribbeana* vol 1 (1910).

Bap and bur 1678-9: PRO Kew, in CO1/44; printed in J. C. Hotten, *The Original Lists of Persons . . . who went from Great Britain to the American Plantations* (New York, 1931). Another copy: Guildhall Library, Ms. 2202/1.

Mar and deaths 1783-9: printed in *Caribbeana* vol 3 (1914).

Births, mar and deaths 1805-18: printed in *Caribbeana* vol 1-2 (1910-12).

Methodist mar 1830-4 and 1857-86: School of Oriental and African Studies.

For registers (from 1637) held locally enquiries should be addressed to the Department of Archives, Bridgetown, Barbados. See C. J. Stanford, 'Genealogical Sources in Barbados', in *Genealogists' Magazine* vol 17 no 9 (1974).

Cuba

Mar 1842-9: PRO Chancery Lane, in RG33/155 (index in RG43/7).

Dominica

For registers (from 1730) held locally see E. C. Baker, *A Guide to Records in the Windward Islands* (Oxford, 1968).

Dominican Republic

Births 1868-1932, mar 1921-8, bur 1849-1910, deaths 1874-89: PRO Kew, FO683/2-6.

Grenada

For registers (from 1784) held locally see E. C. Baker, *A Guide to Records in the Windward Islands* (Oxford, 1968).

Guadeloupe

Military bap 1813-14, mar 1813-15, bur 1813-14: extracts printed in *The*

For addresses of repositories see page 2

For other sources which may relate to places on this page see 'How to use this guide' (page 1)

Genealogist vol 1 (1877), and re-printed in *Caribbeana* vol 1 (1910). The original vol from which these extracts were taken is now part of the Registrar General's military records at St Catherine's House (see page 9).

Haiti

Births 1833-50, mar 1833-93, deaths 1833-50: PRO Kew, FO866/14, 21-2.

Births 1870-1907: PRO Kew, FO376/1-2.

Jamaica

Mar 1666-79: British Library, Add. Ms. 21,931; printed in *Caribbeana* vol 1 (1910).

Mar and deaths 1796-1800: printed in *Caribbeana* vol 4 (1916).

Births 1814-48, mar and deaths 1779-1848: Guildhall Library printed books section, typescript entitled 'A collection of extracts from Jamaican and other newspapers relating to Jamaican families', S917/292.

For registers (from 1664) held locally enquiries should be addressed to the Jamaica Government Archives Office, Spanish Town, Jamaica.

Montserrat

Bap 1721-9 and 1739-45, mar 1721-9, bur 1721-9 and 1739-45: PRO Kew, in CO152/18,25; printed in *Caribbeana* vol 1 (1910).

For registers (from 1771) held locally see E. C. Baker, *A Guide to Records in the Leeward Islands* (Oxford, 1965).

Nevis

Bap, mar and bur 1716-24: Lambeth Palace Library, in Fulham Papers vol 19. Microfilm copy available at Guildhall Library, Microfilm 374. Printed in A. F. Winnington Ingram and S. Phillips, *The Early English Colonies* (London, 1908); also (with omissions) in *Caribbeana* vol 2 (1912).

Bap and bur 1726-7, 1733-4 and 1740-5: PRO Kew, in CO152/16,21,25; printed in *Caribbeana* vol 1 (1910) and vol 4 (1916).

Bap 1729-33 and 1742-1800, mar 1729-37 and 1742-99, bur 1729-40 and 1742-99: printed in *Caribbeana* vol 1-3 (1910-14).

For addresses of repositories see page 2

For other sources which may relate to places on this page see 'How to use this guide' (page 1)

For registers (from 1728) held locally see E. C. Baker, *A Guide to Records in the Leeward Islands* (Oxford, 1965).

St Christopher (St Kitts)

Bap 1719-1823, mar 1724-1821, bur 1719-1821: British Library, Add. Mss. 34,181, 41,178, 41,295, 43,743 and 43,866.

Bap 1721-30, 1733-4 and 1738-45, mar 1733-4 and 1738-45, bur 1721-30, 1733-4 and 1738-45: PRO Kew, in CO152/18,21,25; printed in *Caribbeana* vol 1 (1910).

Bap 1729-1814, mar 1729-1832, bur 1729-1802: printed in V. L. Oliver, *Registers of St Thomas, Middle Island, St Kitts* (supplement to *Caribbeana* vol 4; London, 1915).

Bap 1732-1831, mar 1732-1828, bur 1733-1829: printed in *Caribbeana* vol 6 (1919).

Mar and deaths c.1755-1819: printed in *Caribbeana* vol 3 (1914).

Births, mar and deaths 1839-40: printed in *Caribbeana* vol 2 (1912).

For registers (from 1730) held locally see E. C. Baker, *A Guide to Records in the Leeward Islands* (Oxford, 1965).

St Kitts: see *St Christopher*

St Lucia

For registers (from 1770) held locally see E. C. Baker, *A Guide to Records in the Windward Islands* (Oxford, 1968).

St Vincent

For registers (from 1802) held locally see E. C. Baker, *A Guide to Records in the Windward Islands* (Oxford, 1968).

Tobago

Bap, mar and bur 1781-1817: printed in *Register of Baptisms, Marriages and Burials in the English Protestant Church, Tobago* (anon.; Port of Spain, Trinidad, 1936) (not available at Guildhall Library).

Trinidad

Births and bap 1851-2, mar 1850 in 'International memoranda' at Guildhall Library: see page 6.

For addresses of repositories see page 2

For other sources which may relate to places on this page see 'How to use this guide' (page 1)

Virgin Islands

For registers (from 1810) held locally in the British Virgin Islands see E. C. Baker, *A Guide to Records in the Leeward Islands* (Oxford, 1965).

Many entries for the Danish (later U.S.) Virgin Islands among registrations for Denmark and its colonies in 'Miscellaneous' series 1826-1951 at PRO Chancery Lane (see page 8).

For addresses of repositories see page 2

For other sources which may relate to places on this page see 'How to use this guide' (page 1)